LION HEARTED LOVE

LION HEARTED LOVE

Rising to the Challenge of Money-in-Relationship

MARK BUTLER

Hwy 61 Press

Also by Mark Butler

Zen Money Blues

for Maria

LION HEARTED LOVE

ESSAY III - OPEN BOOK

ESSAY IV - BRASS TACKS

POST-AMBLE

ESSAY

I

THE KULA
OF MARRIAGE

Chapter 1 Death of Certainty

The generation of my American grandparents, like the host of generations before them, may have had all the Answers to money and career and duty and family and courtship and marriage and property and gender roles, but that Certainty had its limitations, its price and, finally, its demise. Date of birth for that Certainty is centuries old, rooted in patriarchal English society and law. Date of death for that Certainty takes place sometime around the Beatles' soon-to-be-mentioned uncouth behavior. There were many little deaths and then one big death. Along the way, great freedom and great confusion were unleashed. This could not be undone.

The death of Certainty is a modern story, really, 40-odd years young, with scant precedent. In our information-saturated modern world it's easy to forget that fact. The situation is fresh! 45 years ago we had Certainty. No one wrote a book about the wild mix of love, money, and relationship because it wasn't *up*. But now it is! The modern agenda for marriage is ambitious. Based on equality, it is to be a partnership of both romantic love and robust economy. People, young and old, cohabiting or marrying for the first, second, or third time, seem up for the challenge. Still, the undertaking is formidable. Money, economy, and the kitchen sink side of life are demanding. Love is no small shakes, either. Bringing them together in a personal and authentic way—well, the ways and means of that are far from obvious. That's why it's the subject of this book.

Not long ago, America was a radically different place. Let the following vignettes serve to remind us of whence we come. The first concerns my American grandmother, circa 1968. She was a lovely and complex woman who was not so fortunate in a marriage where romantic love withered in the shadow of the traditional patriarchal setup. The second story concerns my parents. It is appreciably more uplifting. So named "The Great Fight of 1971," it covers a week-long tussle between my mom and dad. Since it took place at the dinner table, my siblings and I had front row seats. It was intense. It was amazing. It was prophetic. And before I say another word, *Turn that music down. Grandma's home!*

SIGN OF THE TIMES

Rye, New York (1968) – Grandma Millie had not been herself lately. My sisters called them funks, and Grandma all of a sudden had a bad case of them. Mostly, they were an afternoon occurrence. In the morning she was the Grandma we knew and loved. At the breakfast table she smoked her Kent cigarette, drank her black coffee, worked the crossword, nibbled on rye toast with the butter spread thin, and let the ash on her cigarette get really long. At that hour she was a grandmother of few words and she had a small wonderful smile, like a small green apple. But later in the day right around teatime, there would be the smell of that open tin of Scottish butter cookies, and this was the tip-off. Then it was only a matter of time. Something as simple as the mailman pushing mail through the front door slot or a song coming on the radio would set her off. Of late, her ire was directed at the Beatles. This was unexpected. Always Grandma had liked them. *Such fine young men.* Now, no more. After the Beatles went to India, grew their hair long, and published *The White Album* (the cover of which my older sisters peeled away, in search of the band in the nude), Grandma Millie shook her head. Vigorously and often. My sisters said her head might fall off. They even liked keeping count of Grandma's headshakes. Still, these afternoon scenes were best avoided. Easier said than done, though, since Grandma lived with us.

That summer, day by marching day, Grandma's disapproval of the once straight-laced Beatles intensified. One particularly lively afternoon while we were kept inside by electrical storms, we could feel it all coming to a head; Grandma was taking unusually long intense drags on her Kent cigarettes instead of letting them burn down in the ashtray like sticks of industrial incense. *Happiness is a Warm Gun* was playing loudly on the turntable, care of my sisters, who were dancing about the room. Grandma liked to see my sisters happy. Nonetheless, she unloaded, albeit in a hushed tone, at me: *The Beatles are everything that's wrong with these times. Mark my words.* She said it like it was news, and I nodded. What else for a kid to do? That Grandpa Bill was coming to my cousin's wedding in a few days accompanied by his "new" Japanese wife; that Grandpa and Grandma would be in the same room for the first time in ten years; that Grandpa had humiliated her by the conventions of their time—that all of that might figure in to Grandma not being herself was well beyond my ken. We were just kids then, and inclined to think that our life would have been a whole lot easier if the Beatles had just stayed clean cut.

. . . .

Three years later, when the moment arrived, when Certainty came gasping and begging for refuge in our house, amid life in our idyllic New England-esque town, Mom would give it no quarter. This caught Dad unawares. He rather liked the Old Boy. Naturally, a minor dispute ensued. It all seemed harmless enough. Dad never lost this kind of argument. Except...

THE GREAT FIGHT OF 1971

Change was one long unstoppable train of death and birth, riding on invisible tracks that led to who knew where. Electric. Emotional. Exciting. Scary. Most all the movements afoot were way beyond my comprehension, but the Great Fight of 1971 wasn't. I'm not referring to the first Muhammad Ali v. Joe Frazier fight on March 8, 1971 at Madison Square Garden. Indeed, that was a great fight. Maybe the greatest one in my lifetime. But I'm not referring to that. The Great Fight of 1971 took place in the kitchen, between my mother and my father, shortly after my mother declared she was going back to school, to Manhattanville College, to finish her bachelor's degree in Fine Arts.

Grandma Millie recognized where this dialogue could be headed. A sudden peacenik, she beat a quick retreat, taking supper in her room while dialed in to the Merv Griffin Show. We four kids had no such luck when asking to be excused. We of course were central to Dad's argument for more of the stay-at-home gig for Mom. Through 14 rounds (the "discussion" ran through a week's worth of family dinners and desserts), Mom was not to be dissuaded. Finally, Dad went to his go-to 1950's-approved patriarchal move, and delivered what should have been the decisive blow: "Over my dead body are you going back to school!" And Mom did not flinch. Her calm silence and rosebud mien said it all: *Then so be it!*

The patriarchy fell that night, in the summer of 1971, at least in our house. The patriarchy fell hard. It was startling to behold, to see Dad lose the heavyweight championship of our household. Nothing was ever quite the same. No doubt, this happened at countless dinner tables across America, weeks and months before and after, from suburb to heartland to big city. The established roles and rules were on trial. This included the marital contract. Heretofore, society had set and maintained rules and norms that bestowed upon men legal power, economic might, and a bevy of approved social conventions that gave them the upper hand. Like it or not, this inequity served a stabilizing and unifying function. Whether in the home or on the throne, one singular sovereign has a manifestly easier time of it than two ever-negotiating sovereigns. Unilateral decision making is more expeditious, which in no way is to assert better.

This, we know. The nexus of intimacy, ego, power, money, love, and family roles is terribly complex. In a way it probably always has been. But the old order had a built-in escape clause, a put-a-cap-on-it default ending wherein The Man of the House said: "That's it. I bring home the bacon. I'm the master of the household / the lord of the manor / the keeper of this humble abode. My mind is made up. We shall discuss this no more." Peace and order returned. Sort of. The disagreement ostensibly went away. The family and the couple carried on. But at what cost to love, friendship, respect, equality, and self-esteem?

By 1971, that decades-on faux peace was out. What had never fully been brought to resolution, now had to be brought to resolution. Everyone had to dig deeper. Love mattered. Individual happiness mattered, and many more individuals in American society now mattered. Equal status in marriage mattered, even if it wasn't clear what that meant. Economic might was not automatically allocated to the man. Default to dad was over. Everywhere it was over: at home, at work, in the court system. Agendas and roles were to be negotiated, for better and for worse, for richer and for poorer. New answers and new ideas about being life partners called for creativity, and were initially awfully hard to come by. By the early 1980's, the divorce rate basically doubled from where it had been in the mid-60's. Then for these past 30 years it has systematically fallen.[1]

I don't think the return to a more modest rate of divorce is mere slight of statistical hand.[2] In this post-Certainty period, some marriages are clearly working. To be sure, there are intact marriages that are emotionally distant, functioning more like two silos than an ensemble; nonetheless, there is a significant number of relationships where the various rich elements of modern love— of independence *and* interdependence—are coming together. In my personal and professional life I see a willingness of folks to try on new solutions, even if that means taking on substantial economic risks. This seems to be especially the case when there already is a great wealth of love between partners. This risk-taking may be foolishness, genius, or somewhere in between. This may augur financial disaster, greater stress, or good fortune. Only time will tell. No doubt, my observed circle of friends and acquaintances is a statistically irrelevant sample size. Fair enough. But the underlying theme is unmistakable: Couples are being creative in regards to their own situation. Couples are thinking with an open mind about how best to configure the partnership—be it a fresh take on the old forms (you know, choosing a setup akin to Mr. & Mrs. Cleaver); be it a radical expression to the point of revolutionary (i.e., endeavoring to keep up with the Sex Pistols); or, be it any of a million mix-and-match combinations in between (say, Ms. Cleaver is the big-time earner while partner, Iggy, tends to home, children, dog—except when Iggy is on tour with the Stooges).

Absurdities notwithstanding, the present thread is this. There have been successes in these past 40 years, and it is of paramount importance that we learn to recognize them, honor them, and perhaps most importantly, understand and discuss them. To do so, we will borrow from economic anthropology. The notion of the *gift economy* and within that, the Kula of Marriage—the central themes of this opening essay—lend us a framework that should prove useful in discerning what in large part underlies these successes. Chances are very good that said successful couples have—in their own intuitive, emotional way—been smartly attuned to the ways and means of the gift exchange in marriage. Chances are very good they've talked to each other in a manner resonant with the gift economy. It's why the *Lion Hearted Love* discourse will not posit finger-wagging dos-and-don'ts. Rather, it will concern itself with grokking the underlying logic, the state of emotional intelligence, the implied worldview, and the sense and sensibility of the gift economy and the Kula of Marriage. Call it the practical wisdom of this work. It has a huge say in determining relationship victory v. relationship defeat.

Chapter 2   Thinking About the Big Arcs

I am an unlikely bard. Never could I have imagined I'd gather such a trove of richly human stories. But my investment advisory and wealth management practice has afforded me just that—a vantage point, not only in regards to how folks make an array of important financial decisions, but also how those decisions play out over time. Something similar can be said about my experience as a friend and member of the Shambhala, Waldorf, and greater Boulder communities. Folks have at times sought my assistance and shared the details of their personal plight. Now, no personal confidences will be compromised—as is only right—but I mention this because it is what I've been steeped in, because it has created some sort of ripening in my mind-stream, because some matters can only come clear with the passage of time. So, this is where we commence our journey of *Lion Hearted Love*, and this is where we'll repeatedly return, thinking about the big arcs of married life, of what that means in terms of the give-and-take that is marriage.

This opening essay of *Lion Hearted Love* is a wisdom essay, offering up a framework for us to make sense of what is actually going on in the sacred and earthy partnership of marriage. What good is a book that only addresses the finances but doesn't integrate it with the very real, living relationship side of things? What good is financial success if, along the way, we fail to buoy the relationship? Thus, we start here. We aim to understand the very spirit of the partnership itself, as well as the everyday mechanics of it. Without that, there's no stability. Without that, we have no vision.

The organizing principle and metaphor of this opening essay is the Kula, the Melanesian gift circle and gift exchange. It is a beautiful expression of what ethnographers have called the gift economy. I believe this is *the economy* that rightly governs the love-infused marital partnership. Or so I will argue. For the gift economy offers us a vital alternative worldview that lets us account for elements of both the heart and the material, the emotional and the overtly economic, as well as the myriad sacrifices of Self that are done for the benefit of the relationship. In marriage, we recognize this as the proverbial give-and-take. Only the proverbial is no more. The old Anglo-American patriarchal prescriptions of give-and-take expired some 40 years ago. Virginia Slims, baby! 1971! Certainty died. Patriarchy died. But the notion of *marriage as an agreement, an understanding, a contract to be honored* has not.

Today the contract of marriage is free-form. It is the product of our own creation. On the downside, this freedom makes for chaos and confusion at every turn. On the upside, it invites marriage to be a deeply creative act, where reconciling the rowdy mix of love and selfhood and equality and shared economic goals is workable, where the journey is uniquely our own. Nowhere in family life is the demand to get it right greater than in matters of *sharing and dividing labor.* Divvying up the responsibilities of earning money, raising children, caring for our aging parents, serving the community, keeping house, cooking meals, and so on—it used to be so easy. Barely a discussion. Ever understood. The dynamic was orderly for the wrong reasons, of course. Gender dictated role. But that was then. Now we'd like to organize our personal world without damaging love, equality, or finances. Such a quest has us thinking in terms of *the gift economy.*

The second half of *Lion Hearted Love* concerns itself with the very practical side of how couples can work effectively together in the realm of personal money—aka managing the family purse. Money can't buy us love, but love can't pay the bills either! Let's raise our game. Let's be our best, though it must be said that rarely will individuals in a given marriage bring the same strengths, or for that matter the same weaknesses. Therefore, who plays what position, who takes the lead in certain activities and decisions, who gets what kind of control in the personal money game really does matter. While the ethos remains relationship-centric, it is imperative that we discern and evaluate individual differences as per saving & spending, planning & implementing, investing, and critical judgment. This is thematic.

. . . .

For whom is *Lion Hearted Love* intended? For starters, it's for that gritty and cheerful crowd who regards marriage as having a *path quality.* You know, our partner has a pretty good hit rate for nailing us on our less than charming stuff, as well as being a great friend and ally to our best self. We of course provide a similar service (free of charge). And when it works, when we more or less do this for each other with some accuracy and kindness, when we clash without grave injury, and when we love without undue reservation, then I believe we are in the midst of some of the greatest riches of this life. For those of us in a relationship like this, let me state the obvious: Risk life, limb, and ego to take care of it. This circumstance is precious. Meantime, money matters remain edgy, unsentimental, and never-ending. Many a great relationship has strained and suffered because of them. That is unfortunate, and unnecessary. We can bring money matters firmly and solidly onto our relationship path. That is *Lion Hearted Love*'s reason to be.

By the by, this marriage-as-path approach also frequently occurs in second and third marriages. I have real respect and appreciation for folks who bounce back from a tough first go, who really dig in anew. And because a certain innocence has been stripped away, oftentimes because money and the give-and-take of their prior marriage were so contentious, these folks display tremendous bravery in addressing immediately and directly the practical side. Legal counsel may even be hired to protect the individual interests of each person. This is not wrong. But it's not enough. We also need a way to wrap our head and heart around what strengthens and supports the activity and the wealth of the partnership itself. *Lion Hearted Love* is just such a meditation. In the fore are the forms of the Kula and the gift economy. As we'll see, they provide a dynamic framework for us to integrate and account for money and economy amidst love and depth of relationship.

DOWNSTREAM

Economy, at its most earthy elemental level, is not about the wealth and resources of countries, companies, or people, but rather it's about exchange. It's about the give-and-take, and in marriage and family this exchange gets very personal. Perhaps nowhere in life do we ourselves get more instinctively protective than in regards to the young people, particularly when they're thinking about getting married or making a serious commitment to one another. I know I do. The stakes are high. I love the young people and I very much want them to get the give-and-take right; that is, right for them. *Lion Hearted Love* is thus also addressed to those of us who—in our capacity as parent, uncle or aunt, godparent or cousin, brother or sister, friend—can be the truly skilled and savvy guide and helper. The phrase "an ounce of prevention" comes to mind. Somehow, we'd like to help the young-and-in-love solve these relationship riddles *sooner*, to hold the substantive dialogue long before extreme measures are needed.

Of course, we don't need to be all perfect ourselves to guide the young people. Wisdom is born of feats and defeats. I was somewhat humorously reminded of this while having tea with a sagacious old friend from college (Liza). The topic of my book (this work) came up. Liza's response was funny and poignant: *Right now my personal life is a bit of muddle. It's hard for me to think too hard about money and relationship, when I have plenty of money and no relationship.* Divorced 12 years now, kids all grown up, financially hitting it out of the park, she nevertheless wonders if she'll ever find—as she put it—*Mr. Semi-Functional Soul Mate.* In fact, she's just letting the whole thing go for now. *I've got good friends. I do have some dating fun every now and again. But it'll make me nutty to try to make it happen. Maybe I always pick the wrong guys. I don't know. What I do know is that it hurt my first husband that I made so much more money than he. He never said anything, but it was always there. And we're modern enlightened people, right? The gender hang-ups weren't supposed to be there. But they were.*

Not surprisingly, the tone of the discussion brightened considerably at the mention of her 24-year-old daughter, whose future holds such promise. While there is no serious guy in her picture now, it's only a matter of time. How then will Liza help her daughter meet love? How will she help her daughter make sense of what to give and what to expect to get in marriage? *When that time comes, I will be there for her, to sort this all out. Money is intense. Working together is challenging. I've made every mistake in the book. Probably in your book! You know, some new language would be helpful here. Mark, is that what your book is going to give me?* (I certainly hope so.)

Final comment on us providing guidance to the younger generation: It is fine for us to initiate this dialogue. Actually, it is recommended. Through no fault of their own, the young people probably won't run toward it. Why? Because courtship is inherently quixotic. During the time when love is electric, many relationship tasks take precedence over realistically dealing with money and economy. This is appropriate. Love and passion and dreams trump the earthy and the practical. Thus, money lies low. Can lie low for long time. Like a sweaty hundred dollar bill, it's buried deep in the bosom of relationship. Inevitably, though, it will make its appearance. Life unfurls in ways we can never imagine. People get real about money at different times for different reasons. Unexamined assumptions about what the give-and-take of marriage is or should be, come out into the light when the moment requires it, and rarely a tick sooner. The fine print of the marital agreement is often *discovered* long after the time of nuptials.

As most of us firsthand know, getting relationship wake-up calls is hardly contained to the time after the honeymoon. That alarm goes off at all hours of night and life. The marriage might be in need of renewal. Caring for aging and infirm parents may represent a change of life course. Someone—at the age of 40 or

50 or 60-something—might want to go back to school. Change careers. Travel. Paint. Pursue the life of the mind, or a spiritual path. Any one of these can throw a real wrench into the status quo. Make a real economic impact, as well. So, this too is the kind of conversation that *Lion Hearted Love* wishes to give language and perspective to. These are the agendas that test the relationship. We all get them. But when we miss the signs, when we fail the test, we might find some unexpected stuff flying back at us. This is what happened to Sir Winston Churchill. All in all, he was a damned fine chap and hero of the first order. But, he also had his less than stellar moments. And this is where we take up our discussion of the gift economy. Shall we, then?

Chapter 3 Love in the Time of the Churchills

In quotidian life each of us knows that buying groceries at the store is a simple and straightforward transaction. There are no emotional entanglements. We acquire no new best friends in the process. We simply pay for the goods and carry on with our day. Call this a micro-expression of the capital economy. In vivid contrast, there is the ever-shifting kaleidoscope of money and love, of careers supported and careers put on hold, of doing the dishes and serving up three square meals a day, of staying up all night with one's coughing child, of choosing to live in a small house in the neighborhood with the good schools, of supporting the less-than-remunerative artistic endeavors of one's spouse, and so on. These dealings are personal. They're predicated on love. We yield because we love our partner, our family, and our shared journey. Think of them as expressions of the gift economy.

Why the framework of the gift economy? Well, what is marriage if not the most intimate kind of exchange—an ongoing exchange where all manner of gifts are offered up, including but not limited to money matters, career support, emotional support, love, affection, the sharing and/or divvying up of responsibilities, doing the scut work of daily life, all of which can entail some level of personal sacrifice. Interwoven throughout is the truth of time. Such offerings and agreements and sacrifices occur not just over days and weeks, but over months, years, even decades. The ways of the New York Stock Exchange won't be much help here, but the ways and means of the Kula—the interisland Melanesian gift circle—I hope you'll find intriguing. Later on, after a few modernizing tweaks, I hope you'll find it relevant to your life, too.

Right now we'll observe the gift exchange in action. Correction: We'll catch Winston and Clementine Churchill at a relationship low point where the gift exchange miserably breaks down. The story gets us thinking in a number of directions. By tracking and thinking about the marriage of the Churchills (and my American grandparents), we'll put matters in an historical perspective. This is imperative. Past is prologue, as they say. The past powerfully echoes in the present. Patriarchy may be dead, but that doesn't mean it's not trying to control us from the grave! Beyond that, the Churchills—as life partners—are inspiring and beguiling. They lived in the time of Certainty, yet managed to have deep friendship and love. This makes them exceptional. They created one of the great marriages of the 20th century, at least to my mind. But this is not to say they had the fairy tale. The intimate and lifelong partnership of the Churchills might be regarded as many things, but it was no fairy tale.

A KULA MOMENT

Kent, England (1934) – Lunch would end with a crash. Right now, however, the moment called for Sir Winston to rise to the occasion. I speak not of his sudden ascent to premiership in Britain's darkest hour (that would come later), but of the test before him now in his marriage. Lady Clementine had received an irresistible invitation. From London she would set sail for India, Australia, New Guinea and its web of neighboring islands (which we, too, will visit), accompanied by close friends, the captain, and an art dealer. Winston himself had gone on dozens of his own such adventures. In what would be six decades of marriage, Clemmie would make but one. And this would be it.

But Winston was being a pill.

It was the moment for him to be supportive of Clemmie. To be happy for his bride of 30 years. Instead, the former First Lord Admiral (that'd be Winston) broadsided her. Carried on over lunch about why she should stop this nonsense, forget the trip, and tend to her duties at home. He needed her! It was a miserable display. Winston then added one deeply unsubtle, parting shot. He called her selfish. Amazing, though not completely. For isn't this just what we humans sometimes do? We're in the wrong with the one we love; but what the heck, we go on the attack!

Lady Clementine had just gotten up from the lunch table and—incensed by this last shot—spun around and in one seamless motion let fly the lunch plates in her hand. They flew straight and true for Winston's head. Luckily, he ducked. Luckily, too, amid the post-crash clatter, Sir Winston figured out the answer and went and begged for Clemmie's forgiveness.

History shows that Winston Churchill, seldom a good student the first time around, did in fact pass the make-up exam. With a healthy shock from some flying porcelain, he dropped his absurd selfishness and reflected on what his wife had done as a matter of course in support of him and the family. *This time* it was her turn. And although he had been rather slow on the uptake, Winston pulled himself together and genuinely wished her well on her big adventure. Peace was restored.

. . . .

You might rightly ask: Just who was this wild woman and where did she get off flinging Wedgwood china at the man who would save western civilization from the brink? Well, allow me a brief accounting of Lady Clementine's relationship track record. After raising four children, after thirty years of setting up and taking down Winston's households in London, after holding together family finances despite her husband being a dreadful spendthrift, Clemmie should be regarded as a rock. After tirelessly supporting her husband in his public life, deftly offering him counsel on the political lay of the land and on the diverse cast of parliamentary characters in post-Victorian England, she appears to us as an astute ally. But politics is not without its bruising defeats, and here she served by turns as nurse and psychotherapist to Winston. Not least, there also were struggles that lay beyond her sphere of emotional and managerial influence. Episodically, Winston got caught in the jaws of what he himself described as that "Black Dog" of depression. All fell to Clemmie then. She alone carried on, running Chartwell, tending to Winston's affairs, in addition to her numerous familial and social obligations. Given all that, I think it fair to say that Clemmie had a rather large sum of good will stored in the relationship bank.

Withdrawing some of that good will, putting it to work, is a relationship moment of truth. How will the request be received? Whether the withdrawal be large or small, it often calls for change; namely, a shift in who is responsible for what, a shift in the focus and agenda of the partnership. This is where our story began. In the English countryside, overlooking the rolling hills and woods and horse country of Kent, Surrey, and East Sussex, a right honorable gentleman was being obtuse and a proud English lady was in no mood for her husband's antics. She would not beg him to pause and take stock of *who* had selflessly brought *what* to their partnership, no matter how great and important a man he was. What normally would have been a pleasant and quaint lunch for two instead turned into a storm. Bolts of china flew, thunder clapped. Fortunately, Winston and Clemmie had a trove of love.

Indeed, their marriage would last till Winston's death did them part, and it included the kind of storm just recounted. Any good marriage has such storms and, most importantly, moves through them. Then we prune back our ego, and learn and grow as people. That's what we do for love. Winston and Clemmie—they adored one another. Their terms of endearment were silly as a country love song—Mr. Pug and Mrs. Cat. Distance did not separate them either, as attested by their voluminous and affectionate written correspondences. Above all, though, they were the best of friends. How else can a marriage renew and reignite and burn bright for so long?

That said, money was an unceasingly thorny issue in their marriage. A lifetime of affection would not solve this. Winston's worldly greatness would not assuage this. The yellow roses in Clemmie's garden would not prettify this. Money was a pain. In this, the Churchills were not alone. Not then, not now. Marriage then may have been graced with love, but likely it concerned itself first with social opportunity, economic necessity, and perhaps lineage. In terms of gender and gender roles, the traditional arrangement was unequivocally patriarchal. Marriage now looks quite different. True love is expected. Equality between partners is non-negotiable. Gender roles are to be determined. This open template for the union of two people—call it marriage, committed relationship, gay or straight—is a welcome development. It also is the source of wild complication.

As best as I can understand the old arrangement, it was the intensity of love—when it did make its appearance in marriage—

that periodically leveled an otherwise unlevel playing field. This was no doubt true for the Churchills. Love made Winston yield. *Sometimes.* Enough times for Clemmie to feel valued and respected as a real partner in the relationship. But the old arrangement was too often abused, taxing the good will that makes any partnership work. Look no further than Bill, my American grandfather. He had an ego as big as Alaska. Yielding was not in his relationship vocabulary. Still and all, he and Grandma loved each other and worked well together, so much so that—quite apart from the Churchills—money *per se* wasn't the challenge. It was prosperity! For, it was prosperity that amplified their differences and demanded more of Grandpa than mere high-handedness. But this is a sidebar. Let us first get versed in the ways and means of *the gift,* and how it interacts, complements, and at times conflicts with the more culturally prevailing sense and sensibility of the capital approach.

Chapter 4   If Love, Then the Gift

The preindustrial Melanesians and Native Americans seem to have known quite a bit about the workings of what has been referred to by ethnographers as the *gift economy*. They seem to have known quite a bit about not just the material things that changed hands, but what lay behind and beneath such exchanges. Arguably, their genius was social intelligence. For the gift economy, via its norms and protocols, was concerned with how prosperity and good fortune and material goods can also be a source of relationship connection, relationship enrichment, and community renewal. I'm not saying this is the new gospel for modern America to culturally adopt. More, I think the logic and emotional intelligence of the gift economy is a necessary and critical counterpoint to our current cultural approach. Thus, without further ado, without manipulative accusations or dishes taking flight, let us voyage to 17th-century New England, where we'll pay a visit to the Native Americans and Pilgrims; and then, as Lady Clemmie Churchill once did, we'll continue on to the archipelagos of the Western Pacific. Forgive me if we travel *economy class*.

THE GIFT

Lewis Hyde's big two-hearted essay, *The Gift*, begins with an anecdote on the origins of "Indian giver," long a favorite of name-callers and finger-pointers. While neither my children nor their companions employed the term, I do recall hearing its usage back in my day. Hyde of course wasn't referring to the mundane scuffles of my youth, but was taking us back to the time of the newly arrived Pilgrims. That would be 350-plus years ago. As misfortune would have it, the name stems from the gift of a pipe. *No good deed goes unpunished,* are the words that spring to mind. Circa 1640, somewhere in the woods of the future Commonwealth of Massachusetts, an Indian tribe was trying to make nice with its new English neighbors. Things did not go so well. The gift was made to the English, some stretch of time passed, and then the Indians got antsy and sent a messenger to inform the settlers that they'd held onto the gift pipe long enough. Peeved, the Pilgrim leaders—I imagine—spun their modish hats round and round atop their balding heads and said: *How can a gift be a gift if you have to give it back?* From this was born the pejorative, Indian giver.

The righteousness of the English judgment is something many of us can easily relate with today. It seems reasonable to be put off by someone giving you a gift and then later expecting it back. You, I, and the English probably agree on this: Once given to us, the gift property is now ours to do with as we please. This is perhaps THE unwritten rule of our Anglo-American informal gift culture, going back hundreds of years. At Christmas time or birthdays or bar mitzvahs, no one needs to call the attorney or peruse Barron's Law Dictionary to ascertain and assert their "right to possess, use, and dispose of a thing..."—that is, their newly received gift property. That'd be pretty uptight, don't you think?

Yet how the Indians behaved should not be immediately dismissed. The first rule of *their* gift institution is: The gift moves. This is not a wholly foreign concept to us, either. Consider the time of courtship. Between lovers there is a gift fest. Notes, poetry, flowers, dinner, wine—myriad "thinking of you"-isms—and dare we add in gestures of affection, handholds, kisses, embraces, and the highly charged amorous moves. Back and forth. Give-and-take. It's the best. Each day we awaken and offer our best self to our beloved. We listen attentively, we check our self when we talk too much, and we're highly attuned to the subtle signals of communication. We're also highly attuned to reciprocity. Perhaps at first, during that vulnerable time of uncertainty, when our desire that the relationship be good supersedes our ability to take stock—perhaps during that time we blunt our sensitivity around tracking reciprocity, but sooner or later we must open one eye, then the other. If in so doing we find that we're giving giving giving while our beloved—for whom we fervently pine—is receiving receiving receiving, and no subtle hint is going to change this fact, then we've got a problem. No gift exchange, no love.

Returning to the scene of the culture clash of some 360 years ago, the grievance of the Indians is thus: The Puritans, receivers of the gift, took the literal gift property (the pipe) out of circulation. It's a compelling grievance. The Indians' way of gift *exchange* promoted continuity of communication—showing that we are thinking of each other, and ensuring that we will continue to think of each other. In many ways that is the red thread of this particular mode of gift exchange: *I'm thinking of you and, it is hoped, you of me.* The gift exchange is the medium. The cliché, "It's the thought that counts," actually has the potential to come alive. Of course, it's not one static thought that matters. It's the process of exchange—the back and forth of many thoughts, emotions, and gestures—that matters. The Indians had a new neighbor in the English. Bad hats aside, these new neighbors doubtless gave rise to anxiety and uncertainty in the Indians, who did what they do in such situations. They moved closer. They extended. They gave the gift, thereby opening a line of communication with the English. All things considered, this seems like a smart alternative way to try to manage the risks inherent in having a new and strange neighbor. However, the English weren't hip to that. *Nice pipe, thanks.* These English were progeny of the authors of modern private property law and wealth transfer. That they misread the situation is quite understandable. The rest, as the winners always get to write, is history.

Chapter 5 **If Power, Then Capital**

In the world of commerce, the marketplace makes us an offer and we can take it or leave it. At the café where the barista makes our coffee, he is a funny guy but, no, he is not our new best friend; all in all it's a convivial transaction where for three bucks (and a tip) you get coffee and a clean well-lighted place. Emotional undercurrents and heavy expectations are not a part of the transaction. Conversely, the capital-seeking business plan of your spouse is a potential thunderhead packed in an innocent little PDF file. Perhaps you think the plan a lark. *Does the world need another bookstore café?* But then you feel the gravitas. This man is your husband. He loathes his current job, one that he has hung on to these last eight years. He did it to be steady and mature. He did it to be an economic contributor to the partnership. In addition he shops and cooks and does the laundry and in general is pretty handy round the house. Thus you will do well to give the matter proper consideration. *Maybe the world does need another bookstore café!* That he wants to pitch your mom and dad for capital has you feeling queasy. But whatever the case, this is not just another business plan in search of capital. It is family. Yet it is finances, too. In response to this and untold situations like it, many a family member has wondered: Is it possible to deal with this without bloodying relationships or squandering money?

Economy in marriage, like economy in family, has a compelling *interior side*. Sometimes money is just money. Sometimes it's about the subtext, the message imbedded in the exchange. Most often, it's some combination of the two. By contrast, the conventional world of business is primarily objective. *Money is money. You do what you gotta do.* The barista gives you tepid coffee, you send it back. The deal goes bad, you hire counsel to represent your interests. You might think the other guy is a jerk, but it's all in the game. Even in the Mafia—which throws around the rhetoric of being a family, not unlike a few large companies—it's about the money. It's about producing. The "family" rhetoric is all backslaps in the good economic times, but it holds little weight in the bad. Loyalty is an alternating fact of life. When the Mob captain is caught in a betrayal and knows that imminently he'll be swimming with the fishes, he asks one of his old partners in crime to pass along one last message to the new boss: "Tell Mike it was nothing personal—just business." In business, indeed tempers do flare and things do get personal, but to a point. In general, the normative rule we all abide by is that it is *just business* and we should not take dealings too personally.

About a year ago I was reading the *Financial Times of London* and I came across the term *sexual capital*. How perfectly apropos it is of these modern times when fashion and physical presentation and sensuality are all explicitly a part of the game. Of course, the authors were using the term to discuss how sexuality is packaged and presented by individuals (young women, in particular) in the business world, to get the job, to get the deal, to make the key relationships, and so on. In short, elements of sexuality are used for advancing one's interests in business. Like capital, it is employed to garner healthy returns on its investment. Fair enough. But when sexuality is used as a bargaining chip in the inner chambers of a marriage, as a part of a power struggle or to get one's grander agenda put forward, then undeniably that too is *sexual capital*. Whether this is ideal or productive remains to be seen, though clearly it happens all the time. Sexuality is in the service of power. In complete contrast there is sexuality put forward as a generous and open expression of love. That is *the gift*. Same act, decidedly different spirit. And that is illustrative of how economies in home and hearth are *interior* economies: What things mean is very much determined by our intentions. Sex can be about sacred love and intimacy in marriage; or, sex can be about "what I am owed," "the understood deal between us," "what I want," or "what I am not getting."

The capital approach isn't intrinsically antagonistic to relationship, by the way. Nor is it usually enough of a solitary binding factor. It's money, plain and simple, managed according to the most basic fundaments of financial planning: earn, save, spend, and invest. Call it the impersonal side of personal money. On the whole, American couples do seem pretty together on what they wish to accomplish in terms of lifestyle, social status, and expectations around material wealth. Perhaps that's because we live in a society that puts significant time, attention, and care toward capital ends. Perhaps that's a reflection of the "birds of a feather"[3] phenomenon in marriage that sociologists often take note of. Either way, getting the capital aspect of our personal money world right is a significant and necessary accomplishment.

The gift economy is quite different. It concerns itself with the wealth and vitality of the relationship connection itself—in the couple, family, friendship, group, or community. Capital economy is about individualism and personal power. The gift tilts the other way. Necessarily, each couple strikes a balance of the two. We all need power. But in what measure? If we don't have enough, we can feel hemmed in and frustrated in our life. If it's all we pursue, though, it may bankrupt the important relationships in our life. Something similar is to be said for love. We all need it. But as noted earlier, love won't pay the bills. The couple with the richest and deepest emotional connection in all of christendom, for example, still won't be able to use that currency to pay tuition for Jane Jr.'s college education. So, each couple pursues what it deems to be the right mix of capital and gift. This is a personal equation, one that the couple will assuredly refine from time to time.

Apropos marriage, family, and close friendships, I'd like you to think of the relationship as an entity unto itself. It is a vase, a cauldron, a shared psycho-emotional trust account that is neither you nor me—it is the *we* that we both contribute and tend to (or neglect and steal from). Looked at from the perspective of the gift economy's sense and sensibility, a hypothetical couple comprised of two financially wealthy individuals is not therefore a wealthy couple. It depends. Fundamentally, the richness of the relationship—aka the partnership—can be inferred from what also transpires in the gift economy. *What do they exchange, and how often?* Take your pick: love, trust, affection, acknowledgement, generosity of spirit, willingness to share the stress, willingness to share the limelight, kindness, understanding, loyalty, honesty, sacrifice, genuine friendship. These psychological elements are inseparable from the financial. The gift economy brings with it a breadth and depth that naturally attunes to, and accounts for, this part of the relationship equation.

The gift economy is earthy. It happens all the time. When we do someone a favor, there it is. When we give someone the benefit of the doubt, there it is. At birthdays and holidays, it's there. When we turn something intimate (say, a *mor*) into a power spot for emotional punishment or for promoting an agenda, it's NOT there. When we give a gift but just go through the motions, it's not there. Perfunctory is the word; there is no love, no amity, no juice, no medicine. The ritual is empty. The gesture is empty. This is to say: No gift. For the gift is not just an outer action. It requires the alchemy of the psyche. Feeling, intention, and spirit figure in prominently, whereas in the capital exchange those are at best secondary considerations.

I believe we Americans can be quite proficient in making a buck and—when we have our personal financial house in order—getting ahead. In matters of the gift, however, we look out of sorts. Not a surprise, really, when we take into account how restricted the gift exchange in marriage and family has been until, well, 40 years ago. Back in the patriarchal days of Certainty, a man earned a living to put food on the table and a roof over the family's head—that was expected *if* he chose to get married. It wasn't a matter for deep reflection. That's what getting married and having a family meant. What he *wanted to do* was irrelevant. Was it a gift offering to the family that he went hunting (i.e., earned a living), or was he following his bliss? Maybe all that he yearned for was the amassing of wealth and the social esteem that came with that. Then again, maybe not. And what about mom, keeping house, serving up three square meals day after day, and raising the children? Her idea of a good time? Well, you get the drift. In this marital set up there wasn't a lot of room for improvising.

The idea that two married people could negotiate their own way, yield here and get right of way there, was a foreign concept—until it became a sudden and ubiquitous modern concept. So perhaps it does make sense that our forebears could get away with a rather narrow understanding of the gift economy; but today, with the Death of Certainty and the increasing economic equality (by gender) and education tilting in favor of women, all amidst a very strong individualistic bent in American society, I believe this knowledge gap apropos the gift exchange just won't do. More to the heart: IF there is love, IF two people truly love each other, then mastering the modes and nodes of the gift economy is absolutely essential. It really becomes THE money-in-relationship game.

For, love is the amplifying and sublime chemical in all this. A purely capital view of money-in-relationship, by its very nature, will not properly impute the bandwidth of human love, of emotions amplified by intimacy and history, of intuitive and spiritual calls to action. A purely capital view cannot properly make sense of the ordinary or peculiar algorithms of personal sacrifice and family teamwork. Nor should it. The gift economy gives us another look, however. Another way of seeing. Another way of tracking and counting. Obviously it will never once and for all dispel the chaos that is money-in-relationship, but, hey, let's celebrate the small victories, the moments when we do achieve orderly chaos, when we ride the energy of the situation instead of the energy of the situation always riding us! And let's take pride in those victories, too!

Chapter 6 Love and Theft

Science & technology was not their strong suit. The laws were oral, not written. Notions of democracy, the nation-state, and fierce individualism were yet unknown. On matters of the gift, though, they could write the book. I speak of the preindustrial cultures of the Native Americans, whom we just visited, as well as the Melanesians of New Guinea and the Trobriand Islands, who (through the literature of Malinowski, Mauss, and other ethnographers of the late 19th and early 20th century) appear to us as committed and sophisticated in the way of the gift as we in America are in matters of capital. These nations of people took great care in tending to the *relationship wealth* of families, and the social and spiritual wealth of the greater community. The gift economy was seemingly ever on their minds and imbedded in communal and family ritual. Theirs was an evolving communal work of art. The rules and customs that regulated behavior in the gift exchange came down to two:

1) The gift moves. The gift stays in circulation.
   (Do not hoard the gift.)
2) The gift is to remain gift property, and not
   be converted to capital.

In matters of marriage and partnership, I believe these rules—these relationship signposts—are worth keeping in mind.

Earlier, the Native American sense of the gift exchange clashed with the worldview of our Puritan forebears. The pipe, regarded as literal gift property, was taken out of circulation and the Indians objected. As per the latter rule, where the gift is to remain gift property (i.e., the property of the relationship, the family, the community) and not be converted to capital (i.e., for one's own ends, tempting though this always is)—any young chap with half a clue knows that his social stock goes up dramatically the minute he has a girlfriend. But will he try to cash in on this newly revised valuation? In the movie *Sex, Lies, and Videotape*, the libidinous male antagonist (John) does just that. On the phone with a college buddy, he twirls his wedding band and brags about his latest binge of extramarital sexual conquests, "If I'd known … I'd have gone out and bought me a ring when I was 18 and saved myself a lot of time and money." It doesn't take Dr. Freud's (or Dr. Ruth's) analysis to see where this relationship is headed. John, of course, will keep his wife in the dark for as long as he can. He is taking the love and support and care and security of his relationship, spending it elsewhere, and bringing nothing home. It is a deeply unsubtle example of non-integrity in the gift exchange in relationship. In a phrase, *love and theft*.

I have just come from a wrenching two-hour consult with a woman whose husband of 31 years has left her for a younger woman. Allow me to recount the short version. Elegant and educated wife who supported her ex-to-be through law school, raised two precocious children through thick and thin, maintained a beautiful and cheerful home, and served her husband in the old school 1950's style—this is Ellie and she has been unceremoniously dumped by Ed. He left a typewritten note on the kitchen counter, saying he was leaving, and he signed his full name at the bottom. The worst kind of wince material.

Is there more to the story? There always is. Could Ed have felt shut out from the emotional closeness Ellie obviously shared with her two sons and the two grandchildren? Could Ed have somewhere along the line sought to rekindle the fire of their passions, but ended up feeling subtly rejected and alienated in the process? Definitely possible. Relationships are terribly complex, as we all know. But here's the problem with feeling better about the excuse of relationship complexity. What has happened to Ellie happens with alarming frequency in our culture. In former times, uxorial support was all too often met with the husband's careless adolescent behavior. The issue now plays differently. It's increasingly gender neutral, but the overarching dynamic is the same. The *gift offerings of support* by one partner to the other are still frequently forgotten, ignored, or discounted. Sooner or later that is sure to lead to partnership breakdown.

Did Ed use the psychic and economic property of the relationship for his own selfish ends? If so, then he's guilty of *love and theft*. Or, is he guilty of something more basic, though nonetheless hurtful—leaving his marriage in brutish fashion? If so, one can argue he should have had the courage to properly end what he felt was an unhappy marriage BEFORE getting a girlfriend, BEFORE leaving a callous note on the kitchen counter. Was he acting as a shameless thief or an unhappy bloke? We'll never know for sure.

There are funky stories from other quarters, of course. Just this winter past I found myself at dinner with a buddy from growing up who gave a blow-by-blow account of how his ex-wife left him; how for years he felt emasculated because what he had financially brought to the table of their marriage had never been good enough; and now she wanted her independence from him and the boys. *It would have been nice to know all this before we got married, before we had the boys—though I wouldn't trade the boys in for the world.*

But enough he said/she said. Enough he was a fool/she was spoiled stories. The fact of the matter is: Family life in this modern and mobile era is so dang demanding. The weight of earning a living, staying true to our self, caring for our children, nature, art, friendships, and spiritual life, not to leave out tending to the never-ending making of a home—is considerable. The stressors, some of them years-on stressors, can rob any one of us of common sense and critical perspective. People can grow apart—good people. They can also be very generous and giving to the relationship, yet over time can miss what the other is bringing to the relationship. The latter is deadly. It makes good folks stop giving. The negative progression can be subtle.

Many gift offerings for the sake of the marriage and the family are easily lost and forgotten. No evil here, just the nature of the gift exchange. After all, gifts of the day-in and day-out variety (i.e., tending to the kitchen sink) may stop looking like gifts. Other gifts, such as those in the *supporting others* realm, may span over years. They are characterized as much by what that person does as by what she foregoes (i.e., personal sacrifices). The passage of time and a busy, frenetic world conspire to sometimes make the supported spouse forget. Sir Winston forgot. How could he forget? How could he be such a clod? Who knows, he just forgot. Clemmie remedied that, as we know. As important, Winston was remediable!

I am not of the school that says marriages should stay together at all costs. The matter is complicated and no sound bite will suffice. But I do believe Ed should have left his marriage in a way that at least respected and honored what he and Ellie were able to accomplish together in their partnership of 30 years. Besides, divorce will not sever all aspects of the old partnership. They still have children and grandchildren, and those are ties that never stop binding. I wish Ed had been less adolescent and had thought about that.

In this day and age American divorce courts no longer find relationship "fault" with one partner or the other, but they do as a matter of course acknowledge and honor the economic reality of partnership in marriage. Still, if American law serves to guide at the time of marital dissolution, ideally fairly divvying and distributing the so-called marital property, then what serves as a practical guide in the time of love? The economics of love—aka the gift economy—has a complexity all its own. Gifts might be of the straightforward variety, easily tracked, easily counted. *I'll hang with the kids tonight. Go out and have fun with your girlfriends.* Gifts might be celebratory. *Happy birthday! Here's a little cash so you can paint the town red!* Or, gifts might be of the elliptical sort, with twists and turns that cover many miles over many years, as alluded to earlier. The traditional Melanesian gift circle—*the Kula*—has a template for money, economy, love, and relationship that may just serve as that practical guide. Don't be fooled by exoticism, however. The notion of the Kula is direct and no-nonsense. It's there when you do the dishes. It's there when you go on holiday. It's there when you change Little Baby's fantastically messy and odoriferous diaper. It homes in on the give-and-take that is marriage. Done well, it's the perfect antidote to *Love and Theft.* Done well, it's especially good luck.

Chapter 7 The Kula of Marriage

The Kula is the archetypal gift circle practiced between and among the tribal Melanesians of Papua New Guinea and its archipelagos. The early 20th-century ethnographer, Bronislaw Malinowski, spent considerable time there, particularly in the Trobriand Islands to the north. He offers what has become an enduring Western account of the Melanesians and their tribal economics. To be sure, barter was the main mode of commerce; the necessities of daily living were constantly traded back and forth. But weaving in and around and throughout such dealings, there existed another—quite distinct—economy. That was the Kula: the ritual gift exchange of necklaces and armbands that were made of shell. Moving among tribal members on the various islands, the gift made one full circle in anywhere from two to ten years. "A person who participates in the Kula has gift partners in neighboring tribes," Lewis Hyde notes. "If we imagine him facing the center of the circle with partners on his left and right, he will always be receiving arm-shells from his partner to the left and giving them to the man on his right... Of course, these objects are not actually passed hand to hand; they are carried by canoe from island to island..."[4] Eventually, the gift comes full circle to the giver; but in what form and at what time, he knows not. Moreover, the natural flow of the circle ensures that the gift turns a corner, passing out of the sight of the giver. I believe this years-on dynamic of gifts passing out of sight provides a compelling analogy to what transpires in marriage and family, particularly as concerns the long-term projects of launching careers and raising children.

For all the attention devoted to the Kula, you might think we're talking about an inter-island exchange of gold, silver, diamonds, and sapphires, the magnitude of which has pirates lusting. It's anything but. The objects of the Kula—shell necklaces and shell armbands—possess no notable intrinsic or practical value. Shells precious on an archipelago of islands? I don't think so. What is precious, however, is the sociability of the exchange itself. Hyde tells us: "The presence of one of these gifts in a man's house enables him 'to draw a great deal of renown, to exhibit the article, to tell how he obtained it, and to plan to whom he is going to give it. And all of this forms one of the favorite subjects of tribal conversation and gossip'..."

The Kula has its specific normative rules. First, the participant may hold and enjoy the gift for a specified period of time, say up to a year or two, before he makes an equivalent counter-gift in the circle. To hold it longer would universally be considered very poor form. Second, what equivalent gift means is entirely up to the giver. There are neither negotiations nor quality assurance mechanisms. Coercion, too, is unacceptable. As Hyde puts it, "Partners in barter talk and talk until they strike a balance, but the gift is given in silence." Which is not to say that friends and neighbors in the tribe are not taking note. Indeed, there is a chorus of commentary about how the man (or woman) handled the gift, how he honored it, how he held onto it too long or just the right amount; and, how he was generous or parsimonious paying the gift forward. The gift circle told a story for all to see.

Lewis Hyde offers his own list of how reciprocal giving is markedly different from circular giving. The pith of it is this. Giving becomes an act of social faith when we give without being able to see where, when, and how we will one day receive the gift in turn. Control is ceded, undeniably so, when the gift turns the corner. It goes out of sight, and no longer dwells in our immediate sphere of influence. I think a parallel dynamic shows itself in marriage, especially as per division of labor, major family decisions, and life directions. Here, gifts often take the form of personal sacrifices. They are offered for the benefit of the marriage and family, and most definitely "turn a corner," if for no other reason than some endeavors—like launching a career or raising children—take a long time to bring to completion.

THE KULA OF MARRIAGE—MODERN VERSION

Sacrifice, I know, elicits diverse reactions. How a couple with young children divides labor—i.e., who generates some or all of the income, who is primary and who is secondary in caring for the children, who tends to the hearth, and to what degree—is a wild topic. Sacrifices in this intimate quarter could be made actively, passively, cheerfully, begrudgingly, and anywhere in between. Even what constitutes a sacrifice is highly personal and relative to the individual and the family. For example, it is not uncommon these days to learn that both parents want to stay close to home and children, putting their worldly ambitions on hold. That stands in stark contrast to my mother who, after 13 years of playing the 1950's wifely supporting role, was hankering for the world out there!

Where folks decide to live is another major family and life decision. Geography is seldom perfect for everyone. Sacrifice is a common reality, since where one partner thrives economically, the other may feel a social fish out of water; and, conversely, where one partner feels safe and sound in the bosom of community, the other may feel hampered by the economic limitations of the locale. How should such serious and far-reaching decisions be made? That is a subject that deserves its own book. What I can say, though, is that such personal sacrifice is best understood in the framework of the Kula. One partner in the relationship has made a gift offering with a future consideration in mind. That should be honored. That should be held in mind over time. Looming, though, are the risks that it will be lost, forgotten, or taken for granted. The Kula—in its revised, modern iteration—is a powerful antidote to these relationship poisons.

Consider the present marital state of Kevin and Holly, who, early on, discussed and agreed on how to divvy up responsibilities. Now, some 20 years down the line, Kevin has attained great social and business heights, not to mention the charms of the very successful. But he can't recall in the slightest what ambitions his bride, Holly, once set aside in order to raise the children, to make home feel like home, or that she once set aside her individual ambitions. There's no malice on his part, more likely the side effects of a 20-year brutal work jag. What he does know, however, is that he now feels her star—correction, their star—doesn't shine the way it used to, and frankly, he's perplexed.

Kevin is clear on this much, though: He doesn't want a dead marriage. Meanwhile, The Universe, in all its coyote mischievousness, offers him real life pop-quizzes. Some are obvious, some less so. For example, sweeping past Kevin's office every morning is the new hire who knows a thing or two about using sexual capital in the workplace. And while Kevin may sigh, laugh, shrug, or all three, that's the extent of it. The future for Kevin and Holly still holds possibilities. His marriage has lost its sparkle, he knows that, but to him that is not license to abandon it. Accordingly he has accepted Holly's timely invitation to couples counseling. Rejuvenating the marriage is not out of the question. But even if it doesn't make a turn for the better, Kevin has too much respect for Holly to do Love and Theft as his marital exit plan.

Holly's path is worth noting. Coming of age in the late 1960's/ early 1970's, during the last gasps of that patriarchal time of Certainty, Holly was Wellesley educated. As much as the next person, she enjoyed the newfound freedoms and choices of her generation, yet in matters of marriage and family she chose to forego her worldly ambitions and do as my mother originally did: support her husband-in-the-world; love, educate, nurture, and launch the children; and basically hold together house and home. No doubt about it, hers was a gift offering of the first order. This is to say: It was a gift of the self.

This last assertion is far from culturally embraced. American society continues to have a spotty track record in regards to recognizing and properly valuing the supporting player on a team, whether the supporter be male or female. The Death of Certainty provided only a modest boost here. For the record I don't think there is ill will on anyone's part. Rather, it's easier to make sense of the hero—i.e., *the supported*. His success requires ego and pluck and always a bit of luck. Understanding *the supporter* is considerably more difficult. By its very nature such a role is not in the limelight. And success here requires non-ego and inner pluck and great reserves of emotional intelligence. Perhaps you recall how 20 years ago African-American sports stars frequently had the TV camera turned on them after a big play, and what did they say? *Hi, Mom!* Now that's what I'm talking about! Success in partnership is more often than not this union of ego and non-ego. Life seems to demand both. Done well in marriage, this is none other than *the Kula.*

BON-BONS

By the by, I suspect the person in the overt supporter role gets less love and respect than he or she should because of lingering biases about "homemaking." To this day, it still seems to be the case that "what he/she does at home all day" is a mystery. In that public relations void, folks might imagine the worst—i.e., that said *supporter* is home all day eating bon-bons and watching reruns of Audrey Hepburn gallivanting around Rome. Hyperbole? Of course. But the essence of that ridiculousness is what should concern us, because it is born of not really comprehending what the supporter is doing for the family and the marriage.

No doubt the dynamic plays less extremely in the scores of marriages where the supporter role is not relegated to one, full-time person. Since each person supports the other's agenda in a more fluid and daily way, there is naturally more built-in sensitivity and understanding. In the modern iteration, gender roles are also considerably relaxed. The woman is no longer defaulted to the supporting role, although I read quite a bit about how men don't tend to certain matters (like, er, house chores?) as rigorously and conscientiously as their partners, even when they both work full-time jobs. Not sure what to say on that, but I do want to note that even with husband and wife both working-in-the-world, one of them will inevitably fill the bottom-line supporter role when need be. Life is like that. Sick child at school; snow days; tend to sick parents; change air travel itinerary—the list of life's unexpected and inconvenient demands is long. Then, someone's agenda gets put above the other's. Indeed, the person who plays the supporting role these days will often be the guy. I can think of three good friends—two of whom are professionals—who fill that role in their marriage. To be sure, we'll pick up this topic later in our discussion of the *kitchen sink*, that gritty area of partnership where there's really no escaping this reality of supporter and supported, no matter how egalitarian and ostensibly home/career balanced the marriage is.

Returning to the traditionally arranged partnership of Kevin and Holly, she without question has been the supporter. She is the one who has tended to the kitchen sink level of their life. If there were a listing for her job on *monster.com* or in the classifieds, it might start like this: *Looking for someone who can set aside her ego!* There's no denying that hers is a job that won't win headlines or grab big bonuses, no matter how good and steady the performance. Done poorly, though, and everyone will riot, because: somebody has to change the bulb in the night light in the bathroom; somebody has to make the appointment to have the kids' teeth cleaned; to buy the food, to put three square meals on the table; to wash the linens, and attend to the kids when they're sick or when they're blasting the Marshall amp a little too loudly in the basement. Oh, and then there's that not so little thing about helping the young people develop character, become emotionally grounded, and learn to make mature decisions. You get the drift. This is but a brief accounting of Holly's 20 years of "stay at home" activity.

Now Holly is ready to change it up.

One morning not three weeks ago the house was quiet, the kids gone back to college, and Holly looked out her kitchen window and knew she was finished with her full-time supporting role. *How much money is enough? This feels old. I want time with*

Kevin. Have an adventure with him. Have an adventure all my own. Although they had not discussed it, she felt what Kevin felt: Their marriage had become a brown study. Holly's call to Kevin that morning began with the ominous, though sincere: "We've got to talk." It was a call to couples counseling. Kevin was on his marital game. He heeded that call.

. . . .

Given the very nature of the tasks to be accomplished in marriage and family, it is often the case that the request for changing things up may not happen for many years. In the ancient Kula it could be 10 years before the gift returned to you, but return it assuredly would. Everyone knew that. Everyone in the Kula could count on that. Interestingly, such a trustworthy system still required social faith. Gifts that travel over a long arc of time require a tremendous amount of trust. In modern family life, we have no binding Kula framework as of yet. There is little in the way of assurances that the gift, given long ago, given over a ten- or twenty-year period, will come full circle to the giver. It is no wonder a certain modern relationship anxiety persists. Good people are understandably leery of getting stuck in a supporting role in marriage and family. This is a very real issue. This is where the Kula in marriage is instructive.

Chapter 8 Big Arcs of Life and Love— Interrupted!

In the time of Winston and Clementine Churchill, and for that matter of my American grandparents, the terms of marital engagement were clear and not to be fussed with. While this institution no doubt engendered stability, the expected "returns on the marriage" were far from guaranteed. Take my American grandparents. Bill met with success, forgot his sense of noblesse, and became unyielding; in response, Grandma withdrew her emotional support of him. They gained money, yet in the end managed to lose love. By contrast, Winston was maddening how he often ran amok with expenditure, yet he and Clementine managed to not let it ruin their love. Arguably, it was Clemmie's exceptional emotional intelligence and emotional strength that repeatedly put their marriage back on the right track. Because love was honored, because in moments of *relationship truth* Winston yielded power and thus as partners they were ultimately equals, the Churchills did in fact do the Kula of marriage. Alas, the same cannot be said for my American grandparents. Grandpa's insistence on the upper hand poisoned love.

Equal status in marriage today doesn't mean that both husband and wife grow mustaches, share exactly 50% of housework, contribute exactly 50% toward living expense, and, equal opportunity, play cricket on Wednesday night; though it could! How we apply the principle of equality in relationship typically shifts over time. Early on, when the fires of courtship burn bright, the ethos tends toward everybody chipping in. She cooks, he does the dishes. Or vice versa. Time to do laundry? Our fervent lovers declare: Let's do it together! As to the chores of vacuuming, shopping, window cleaning, and the like, they receive similar treatment. The issues of pooling income, financial assets, paying bills, and commingling (or not) personal finances also leap to the fore, matters we'll properly take up in the second half of this book.

Nothing against the super-cooperative approach to domestic life and personal finances; however, at some point this setup gets disturbed. He goes to medical school, she goes to law school; he does his residency with 100-hour shifts, she gets a job out of law school and works 80 hours a week. Much as we all relish harmony and balance, life is full of periods when it is anything but. In response to any one of them, our married couple-in-love may rely on take-out food in lieu of making dinner, or come to frequent the neighborhood restaurant. Then again, one spouse may change by dramatically picking up the slack in domestic matters. Here we see the marked shift from *shared* labor to *division* of labor.

Another game changer: Children. Whether or not their arrival was planned, doesn't matter: Toss all notions of harmony and balance out the window. The goal now is to survive. If at some point you transcend survival mode and recover your sense of humor, you're Buddha. If amidst poopy diapers and projectile vomiting you rouse the occasional moment of elegance in your world, you're Queen of the Realm. If, while the little cherubim takes a nap, you and your partner make passionate love (even though you are more sleep deprived than political prisoners in Stalinist Russia), then you're Venus in the flesh.

For other couples the notion of "children" is metaphorical: Art is their child, career is their baby, Nature is their church, or immersing themselves in a Dharmic life is their 24/7 proposition. Culture, Art, Nature, Career, Dharma, Community Service— any one of them becomes the focal point, the heart center, the organizing principle for their partnership. It is possible that the couple equally shares the same life passion, though more likely one person will be supportive of the other's activities. I want to be clear here that while I make frequent references to *couples with children*, it is obvious that for many couples children are not the binding, catalyzing, or challenging factor. My choice here is rhetorical. Do forgive the limitations of that. It matters not how a couple or family organizes/constellates, or whether they have literal or figurative children; you get the point.

Our topic is the Kula, and within that how couples divvy and share responsibilities. Now a word is in order regarding the literal arrival of children. Today, some folks respond to the challenge of growing a family by choosing the so-called traditional arrangement, where one person is the big breadwinner and the other tends to home and hearth and nurturing the little ones. But, quite apart from tradition, *this arrangement is a choice* and that itself makes all the difference. For many, though, figuring out who raises the kids, who works in the world and how much, how the house chores are tackled is still far from a simple prescription. During 24 years of raising children, my wife and I have employed three or four configurations on sharing/divvying of labor. When the children were very young, we sacrificed earned income for flexible schedules, wanting to be around in those high emotional need years. As the children hit the teen years, we reconfigured with an eye toward optimizing income, since two college tuitions and saving for retirement would soon be staring us in the face. Did it all work? Mostly.

Ours is but one of countless partnership tales. It seems as though couples in every socioeconomic class in America are working this one very hard. Still, it's not easy to get it right, to come up with a formula that gets everyone enough of what he/she wants and needs. And even when we do, it's not forever. What works swimmingly in one period of life, say, when the children are young, might not in another. Or, goals change. Individual goals, relationship goals, family goals. They change because we change or life changes or life changes us, or some combination thereof. A loved one might get sick or die in an accident (sorry to go dark) and suddenly we find we are regularly visited by the Black Dog. We wonder what's really important in life. Wonder whether we've made an existential wrong turn. Such a period of life can radically transform what *getting it right* means.

Perhaps for you, like many others, the destination defines the journey. If you seriously want an upper-middle class lifestyle, for instance, that will weigh heavily on where you decide to live and how you and your partner strike a balance between work life and home life. On the other hand, you may care more about the inner qualities and less about the outer aspects. Extra money would be nice, you both agree, but having ample time for each other and the children is the priority. Or, maybe it's a priority while the children are young. Or, the time premium might hit while your parents struggle with the vicissitudes of old age, sickness, and death. As well, the priority might be nature and simplicity: Thoreauian, if you will. You care to live in the country where Nature is amazing even if the local economy is not.

The variations and trade-offs are endless, of course, and in such gritty real-life matters, it's not easy to keep score of it all. Today's marital agreements are real, yet fluid. Misunderstandings as to who has done what, for whom, and why, provide seemingly endless fuel to marital discord. Think about that. Arguments are often a variation of this keeping score theme: someone feels taken for granted, someone is cross because things feel unfair, or someone feels that the other person "doesn't have a clue what I do for him," or accuses the other of being "selfish." The accused—our partner—will strenuously object to these accusations, naturally. He might even counter with his list of grievances. Then the dialogue can get really heated.

This was true for Pablo and Betsy.

Their struggle seemed straightforward. We all thought Betsy was—for reasons unknown—suddenly acting spoiled and at times disrespectful toward Pablo. We were wrong, however. Act II would reveal a much bigger issue afoot. Betsy had a big life change in mind. Pablo resisted. He was sure he was in the right, moreover, because back in the day Pablo and Betsy had "consciously and deliberately" chosen their roles and responsibilities in marriage and family. But I have said too much. First let's see Betsy cut, Pablo bleed, and us (Pablo's golfing buddies) mercilessly take full advantage of him on the golf course.

PABLO Y BETSY — ACT I

As to what goes on behind closed doors in another's marriage, one never really knows. Pablo's side of the story alarmed us, nevertheless. All day on the golf course he had visibly not been himself. Of course golf friends being golf friends, we placed a ton of bets against him and won a lot of his cash. Afterward over drinks, he acknowledged he was the walking wounded. Just this morning Betsy had reamed him on the phone for coming on the trip. Pablo felt sure he had done everything right to be here. We peppered him with questions.

You planned this in advance, right?

Right.

Betsy knew she'd be with the kids?

Yes.

You got her buy-in months ago?

I did.

What are we missing here?

Nothing that I know of.

Although we all thought it, none of us was fool enough to say it: *If you did do all that, then what's eating Betsy?* Instead, we ordered him a stiff cocktail and left it at that. The conversation returned to golf. Time now to do our own rendition of ESPN SportsCenter, wherein golf is the day's news and we are both the sports commentators and the day's stars. From time to time, this post-game ritual is better than the golf itself. Tonight that was the case. In the end light-heartedness was revived.

Hey, guys. Thanks for putting up with me, Pablo said. *It's such a turn off, this bitter "You get this and I get that" thing that Betsy and I have going on. I don't know how it got to be like that. Betsy knew full well she'd have a house full of kids when I came down here. Business has been nutso for me. I desperately needed this time to recharge. But all Betsy could say on the phone this morning was,* "Wait till you get back. Have I got plans of my own." *Where's the love in that?*

Pablo excused himself, and set off in search of the loo.

His absence provided us, the ad hoc jury, with the opportunity to discreetly compare notes. In two minutes' time we three agreed on the verdict. Tony was pithiest, if a tad indignant. *Does*

Betsy know what a stud Pablo is in business? The guy makes a lot of cash, is humble about it, always considers it theirs. He's not some clown who goes to the office, screws the secretary, and drinks Manhattans—like some dude out of Mad Men. *Jeezuz! Pablo is a stand up guy. If he has a flaw, it's that he makes wheeling and dealing look easy. Betsy doesn't know how good she's got it.*

Pablo was returning and now in earshot.

Tony went diversionary: *How 'bout those Rockies, eh! They look good in spring training. I think they'll be contenders this year...*

PABLO Y BETSY – ACT II

As to the contention between Pablo and Betsy, the golfing guys (myself included) were wildly wrong. We raced to judgment based on incomplete information, and reacted from what was clearly a sore spot for some guys in the modern era—that is, having the value of one's hunting prowess severely discounted. We also managed to completely forget what we already knew: Betsy was a person of character, likable and smart, and there's no way she'd be busting Pablo's chops for petty reasons.

While riding around in a cart with Pablo during a game of golf one month later, I got the rest of the story. Betsy wanted to get to work on a master's degree program in clinical social work as soon as possible. If she enrolled this fall, that would mean big changes for everyone. Pablo: *I'd have to be around a lot more, or suffer the consequences. You know, kids in high school and junior high sure do know how to party at the house with no parents! That means less time for me in my business—which is going gangbusters right now. For that reason alone I hate the thought of pulling back on my time. But really, I'm upset with Betsy. I feel she betrayed me. Way back when, Betsy and I had long series of conversations about her being a stay-at-home mom and me going out and providing for the family. I think she's done a good job for her part and I think I've done a good job for mine. I'd like to keep it this way. So, yes, I am digging my heels in. I don't see why can't she wait till Matt heads off to college, then go back to school herself. That's in six years time. It's not that long.*

Betsy perceived that six years wait time very differently, I'm sure. That most in her peer group intended to wait till the nest was empty before trying to change and chart the new course was not lost on her. Nor do I think Pablo and Betsy did something wrong. Even if the Kula dialogue had been their longstanding *partnership habit,* and thus they stayed current and aware of who was doing what for the partnership, I still doubt it would have prevented this moment from arriving. Change at times is mysterious. Why now? Sometimes that's obvious. But sometimes the call for change arrives in full force, devoid of clear explanation. Was this particular call for change prompted by Betsy's personal psychology? Or, was it in reaction to something out of balance in the relationship, perhaps out of balance for a long time, and all of a sudden she hit her limit and felt the need to change it up? Possibly it coincided with achieving a level of economic success for the family—at least "success" from Betsy's point of view. What isn't mysterious, though, is this sort of intense partnership *interruption* is not exclusive to Pablo and Betsy. It appears at one time or another in a raft of marriages. The timing is often "irrational." Don't be misled by that. Calling it "irrational" is to say it's coming from an emotional, intuitive, or spiritual realm. It's still powerfully real. All the condemnation in the world is not going to make it go away.

For years, Betsy has worked part-time in the world and full-time in her family. That was in accord with their original agreement—the one they had assiduously talked through and together made their own. In so doing, did they ascribe an exact timeline to the chosen roles and responsibilities? No. But it was implied that it'd be "a long time." No argument from Betsy or Pablo on this point. Betsy herself never thought in year 16 of marriage she'd want to make sudden and significant changes. Then again, who among us can intelligently project that far into the future? One thing is for certain: Betsy is not apologetic that she wants what she wants.

Her 16 years of selflessly tending to the *kitchen sink* means— at least in her mind—she has a lot of relationship goodwill points in the bank. Do her 16 years in the supporter role give her the right to call in all that goodwill and set the agenda now? There's no easy answer, of course. But such interruption will assuredly have dramatic consequences, and nowhere more than on the kitchen sink level. For that is where supporters support. They are the ones to whom the majority of unglamorous chores in domestic life fall. Without someone holding this down, day-in day-out, over months and years—home life comes to a screeching (and perhaps screaming) halt. That's what worries Pablo. Can he do it well? Equally, does he really want to do it? His ego naturally wants to run the other way. At the same time, he loves Betsy and doesn't want her to run the other way! Doing the occasional dish is one thing. Having to help your distraught daughter who just had a disastrous day in middle school is something else entirely. It doesn't stop there. Having to not only start the laundry, but finish it—week after week, when he could be watching the Golf Channel without folding clothes—well, Pablo has his reservations. His father as a role model is absolutely no help here. His brother, Jorge, lives with four cats and a cello; his flat has one chair and a music stand; enough said. Just thinking of Jorge made Pablo feel desperate. Maybe his mother could move in with them. *Uh, no, terrible idea!* What then? *I need the manual.* Pablo thought about the matter some more. *And I need some guarantees!*

Chapter 9 The Modern Kula Rx

Taking someone for granted—look, I have nothing profound to say here, only the obvious: Bad idea! Bad habit! No one likes his or her efforts to be assumed as a gift already given. No one likes to be discounted because he is steady and can be counted on. *Making money is easy for him. What's the big deal in that?* That kind of attitude really ticks people off. But most often it's not an attitude. Rather, it's a bad habit born of folks being crazy busy and thus not making the time to stop and reflect and, yes, appreciate what everyone is bringing to the feast. If true, the danger then grows that good people who really do love each other, will unwittingly set in motion a cycle of mutual non-appreciation.

The remedy is basic and cheerful, thank goodness, and it's what a lot of folks intuitively do in the course of date night. That is, they appreciate each other. But at the risk of sounding pedantic, I must say that such appreciation—for our Kula purposes—must be done properly. Sure, doing it "with feeling" is a good idea, but actually there's a thinking component. For appreciation to really mean something, we, the appreciator, need news! Need details! Need updates! Then when we express gratitude, our life partner will take it to heart and feel good about it. The annoying opposite has been aptly and repeatedly mocked in TV shows like *The Office:* The team leader, usually a clueless Group VP in a suit, stands up in front of the group and cheerleads and applauds them with vapid platitudes, all the while the underlings smile fake smiles and mutter, *Spare me the bull, just pay me more!*

Heated arguments in marriage, as we've all experienced, do have a way of clearing the air and rapidly getting us up to speed on the State of the Relationship. Downside to such arguments: They burn and bruise. By contrast, there is the periodic Kula dialogue, aka the Partners Meeting, whereby we get caught up on what all has been done for the partnership lately, and by whom. This seems a gentler way to get current, and stay current. Keeping this dialogue going might rightly be regarded as the core relationship *practice* of the Modern Kula. It possesses two parts. One: We take a genuine interest in the details of what our partner has been up to. Two: We put forward the details of our own activities. Sweetly, straightforwardly, and with just the right amount of ego, we tell our partner what we've done for her and the partnership lately. This is critical. It's not her job to be telepathic, or to ask us questions like a psychoanalyst. She's a busy gal. How could she or anyone possibly know what we really do unless we put it out there, and do so with periodic updates and revisions?

If practiced, the Kula dialogue will enrich. Will incline toward generating cycles of mutual appreciation, the very lifeblood of the Kula of Marriage. No guaranteed happy outcomes, of course. We may learn through the Kula dialogue, for example, that our spouse isn't as thrilled as we are with the prospect of increased income from overtime at the office. No, she'd rather we be home for a million other good reasons. This is where courage figures into the Kula. We have to be willing to hear the truth, or say the truth, and from that place negotiate—as opposed to the non-dialogue mode, where we offer up or receive gifts in silence and don't really know how our partner feels about what is going on. The latter was fine in the communal societies of the preindustrial Melanesians and Native Americans, because the whole village was watching and discussing what was going on. But in modern marriage, where privacy is the norm, where no one in the village is inclined to mind another's marital business, I think giving gifts to the marital partnership *with voice* is responsible and appropriate. Giving in silence leaves too much to chance. Why do that? The Modern Kula dialogue is a partnership practice worth adopting. Usually cheerful, it's ever the means to supreme relationship protection.

Chapter 10 Kitchen Sink

Keeping score in relationship—the idea of tracking and counting the give-and-take—seems like a faux pas. Sounds like the ultimate turn-off. Sounds parsimonious. Uncouth. Definitely sounds like it violates the spirit of the gift. Or, does it? What if we took it and made it work for us and for the relationship? In the last chapter I broached the idea of the Modern Kula dialogue, wherein we not only listen anew to our partner, but we also do some soft self-promotion. It's the "What I've done for you/our partnership lately" dialogue. I imagine the proposition might have sounded odd. But think about it. Don't we post-honeymoon do some version of this relationship accounting already? Aren't many of us displaying this very fact when, amidst a spousal disagreement, we express our displeasure at getting the short end of the stick on something or other? There is some sort of mental tracking device at work and it's telling us to tell Gerard, Bernard, Mike, Mark, Fred, or whatever his name is, to go to hell—i.e., that the goings-on of marriage (and the gift) are not feeling equitable at the present time. This is one way to clear the air, like an afternoon thunderstorm, though it can be exhausting if not perilous.

In the time of Certainty, the man of the house authoritatively laid down the standards of relationship accounting. Was it fair? *It was fair if your father said it was fair, goddammit!* But that's behind us. Looking in the rearview mirror we also see the ancient Kula, where the participants in the gift circle acted while members of the village watched the activities. Who did what, when, and how were much discussed. How people conducted themselves in the gift exchange spoke volumes about their character. The community took note. The community kept score. Modern marriage, in contrast, is an extremely private matter, a life typically out of the view of others. The ultimate integrity of each person in the marriage is rather difficult to assess from the outside. As concerns how to track AND assign value to what is going on, to who is doing what, etc., the couple is left to its own devices. I don't think any of this is a problem, particularly. Keeping count per se doesn't sabotage love, although the question naturally follows: How can we do this artfully? I think the answer falls under The Personal and Deeply Creative header, to be figured out one couple at a time.

Mischief and misunderstanding frequent one particular quarter of family life more than the others. I speak of the *kitchen sink*. This continues to be the severely discounted slice of activity in American family life. Many a gnarly fight erupts here. Some fights go the full 15 rounds. A few of them carry on way beyond the bounds of civility. It's emotional stuff, particularly when there are conflicting views of what it entails, of what value should be assigned to it, as well as vastly different understandings of the sacrifices Some One makes to tend to it. The funny thing about the kitchen sink, which we all know, is that no one notices what it takes to make it work until Some One goes on strike. Then the sink is clogged, the dishes are dirty, and the toilet won't flush.

Family life becomes a mess. Even in less extreme circumstances, where change is afoot and all parties agree in spirit to that change, the impact of possible disruptions is so ubiquitous and far-reaching that it poses tremendous challenges—challenges that none of us can really comprehend until we're in it.

In the beginning, in the middle, and in the end, the kitchen sink is speckled with the unexpected. This makes it a rather asymmetric 24/7 proposition. Betsy could try to explain this to Pablo, but I know her well enough to say she's the kind of person who thinks there's no teacher like experience. Besides, after employing carrot and stick and sundry arts of persuasion, Betsy has brought Pablo around 180 degrees to her way of thinking: She certainly doesn't want to do anything that might undo their new accord! Ah, the venial sin of omission. But even if she made full disclosure, would he, or anyone for that matter, really get it? Betsy knows firsthand what awaits Pablo. As for Pablo, he has most definitely loved Betsy all these years, but no, he's never strained his brain thinking about what she's been up to. Till now.

BUYER'S REMORSE

One night—at 2:31am, as Pablo tells it—he wakes with a start, and wonders what he's gotten himself into. He's haunted by one of Betsy's perennial retorts to him: *You don't know the half of it, Señor Pablo.* The half of *it* he more or less knows pertains to her endless trips to the dry cleaners, the all hours taxi service for their wildly social kids, the hour wait on hold (the hour she did not have) to ask the IRS agent for one small but critical clarification on their recent tax filing, and, not least, performing short-order-cook feats to produce breakfast, lunch, and dinner for five.

An engineer and entrepreneur by day, Pablo now drills into the revised division of labor equation. In terms of house chores and being there for the children, Pablo figures he's been covering about 10, max 15 percent of it. *That number will change!* It's 2:51am and Pablo is formatting data sets in his head as to what it means to replace Betsy. Current working hypothesis: Pablo will be on the hook for about 60 percent of the kitchen sink detail in the new arrangement. *Hmmm. I'm screwed. Funny I never thought about this. Out of the frying pan and into the fire.* Pablo yearns to eat pickles and watch the Golf Channel all of a sudden. *I think there's a tournament on the Australasian Tour. And a new stash of Batampte pickles!*

Pablo chastises himself for getting off track, particularly at this hour. In need of a solution, he focuses on the slow moving ceiling fan, one of his top problem-solving allies. It's 3:19am. *I got it!* Time to hire a cool young person, ideally fresh out of college, to help with the cooking and drive the kids to sports practice, piano lessons, what have you. The cost for said Cool Helper should be feasible. Betsy gets peace of mind, and Pablo the freedom he'd rather not give up. *Seems like a win/win all the way around! All will be good in the kingdom.*

It's 3:39am.

But will it?

Pablo feels in his gut he's still missing key data.

I don't know the half of it, do I?

LABOR OF LOVE

No doubt about it, the kitchen sink aspect of family life is the original labor of love. Grandparents, nannies, housekeepers, and personal assistants can most definitely help manage the situation, but only up to a point—because, in the middle of the night, babies do have a way of shouting out after going poo-poo in their diaper and because, at the worst possible time, teenagers have performed boneheaded maneuvers. We'll add to this list in a trice. But first this comment: The responsibility for dealing with these situations almost always falls more heavily on one spouse than the other. Perhaps this is ridiculously obvious. Except it warrants mention, because some couples fight this truth (and each other) every step of the way. Mostly, though, couples get caught off guard by the sudden necessity to *adapt* to the situation—whether it involves children, a personal health issue, elder parents on the wane, to name a few.

In the case of children and the kitchen sink side of life, there's little let up. For example, when Jane Jr., age 3, brings home from preschool a gomboo of a cold and she's coughing her head off in the middle of the night, Some One is going to pop out of bed and attend to her. But if a negotiation is first required, I think it safe to say it will be an ugly and unharmonious conversation. More likely, the outcome will entail a division of labor. One person is going to pop out of bed knowing full well it falls to her/him. Why that one person and not the other? That will accord with their agreement. Perhaps it's driven by who—when push comes to shove—has the more "important" business the next day. That person will sleep like a slug while the other person ventures out into the cold of night and comforts Jane Jr. for as long as it takes. Needless to say, said Cool Helper is home sleeping peacefully in her bed: She sure as heck will not be getting up in the middle of the night. It is in these moments that it's obvious the once perfect ideal of shared responsibility is a joke.

The kitchen sink side of family life is the original labor of love.

And it never stops. Accosting many a young family are untold variations of the unexpected. Sick children need to be picked up from school. Mother Nature acts out: *Snow day!* And there's no snow day at work for either Mom or Dad. Or, Jane Jr. needs to see the doctor, but Doc's lone gap in the calendar is mid-morning. Then there's the emotional side of family life that episodically shouts out for attention. Your oldest has just had the most miserable day of her life, worse than yesterday (which had been the most miserable day in her life). With a dose of loving-kindness from you, she rebounds; but your youngest now has a strange pallor from too much sugar, not enough sleep, or both, and now he is melting down because the different foods on his plate are touching each other. *Who's going to relate?* Even with Cool Helper in the picture, situations like this happen all the time, and they require that Some One be attentive, skillful, and above all care.

For 16 years Betsy has been that person.

Now Pablo will become that bottom-line person. He has lost subsequent nights of sleep thinking about it. This augurs well. The import of the time is dawning in his mind. The kitchen sink side of family life is not to be taken lightly. When it is, or when folks shirk these duties, then we can safely predict one of two things will occur: A marriage will find itself on the rocks, or a house full of teenagers will be rocking and rolling out of control. Divorce is expensive. Therapy is not cheap, either. Big times, these truly are. Love doesn't get any grittier than this.

Chapter 11 # Best Laid Plans
of Mice and Men...

Some marital arrangements can prove to be extremely effective and profitable, literally and figuratively growing empires and staving off wars. Here, the contract of marriage is put to a decidedly capital end. What matters is that there be ample social and financial return on that marital partnership. *Cynical and selfish,* some moderns will protest. Others will undoubtedly reply, *Dude, it's the way it's been since the world began. Of course people still marry to move up, to gain advantage, to enter social circles that open doors.* At its most extreme the presence of love is beside the point.

Another kind of marital agreement calibrates to the longing for love. The pursuit of status and power are subordinated to what sustains relationship harmony. The journey is characterized by the gift economy. Creativity is called for. Relationship itself seeks to become art, albeit an eternal work-in-progress. Managing the day-to-day responsibilities remains important, obviously. The feelings and intentions behind our activity also matter greatly. If we tend to the kitchen sink side of life as if it's an oppressive J.O.B., then the Kula will break down. Once upon a time, Betsy (of Pablo y Betsy) signed on to be a stay-at-home mom and assumed the role of Vastly Overqualified Attendant of the Kitchen Sink. She did this out of love. She did this out of a shared vision for family—to establish their own social and economic place in this world. But then she changed. Seemingly out of the blue. Pablo cried foul.

What about that? From the rational perspective Pablo had a point. Some might say an indisputable point. A deal is a deal. How can a deal be a deal if it periodically is subject to change? There was no fine print in the marital contract that stated: *Terms to be renegotiated if I loathe what I chose.* Now let me be clear, there are individuals who will manipulate a situation, who will take the easy way out, if that is an option. To which I reply: *Look, if you married someone like that, then flowing with this Kula groove stuff is the least of your problems.* Character is born of the thousand choices we make on the road of life. The Kula is not going to magically transform individuals into People of Character. That integrity is already assumed. It is a necessary precondition. Betsy is a substantial person, with her own brightness, style, and intelligence. This call for change was no case of impulsivity on her part. She'd been doing yeoman's service in the kitchen sink realm for 16 consecutive years.

From another point of view, Pablo—in his initial mode of protest and resistance—was being absurdly unrealistic. After all, *Who signs on to do something forever? And if they do say it is forever, who is silly enough to believe them?* The answer is Lovers, of course. How lovers make a deal is often bereft of business common sense. I know, the idea that we might look to boring old business to do the Kula in Marriage is limited, but in the area of negotiating contracts we should take heed. Go no further than a cup of coffee and my trusty source of inessential news, *Yahoo!*

Sports.

It is October 2011, and NBA management and labor are in heavy negotiations. The existing contract is set to expire. Time to agree on new terms, or risk a strike / lock out. Assuming they make a deal, it won't be *in perpetuity.* The time frame of the legally binding agreement will be finite. This makes sense for all concerned parties. Life changes, markets move, opportunities shift, usually in ways that are not foreseeable. Good agreements, like the best laid plans, recognize limited visibility into the future. The institution of business factors this in. The institution of marriage often does not.

But it should.

Chapter 12 Capital and Gift (Reprise)

B ack in the time of my grandparents and parents, the main cultural focus was on making a buck, getting ahead, and realizing the material side of the American Dream. I don't condescend in making note of this mid-20th-century phenomenon. It was a time of economic mobility and my family, among many, made its move and benefited greatly from the times. Was it a time of duty, service, and respect for authority and tradition? Yes, by and large. Was it a time of original and critical thinking? In the main, no. Which is not to diminish that many families made the proverbial hay while the sun shined in America. Making a buck, providing for one's family, and getting ahead all do have their undeniable benefits. I feel gratitude to my grandparents and parents, whose economic successes opened a world of experience and opportunity for my siblings and me.

It all came at a price, of course. The marital setup, while economically potent, was not conducive to love. It was unequal and inflexible. These days, we have considerable Uncertainty but the trade-off is greater individual latitude, more choices and commitments born of reflection, and countless creative iterations of how to do marriage in a way that keeps it alive, even burning bright. So here we are. No better conditions exist such that the Kula of Marriage can find its own unique expression, one couple at a time. The regard for equal status in marriage is increasingly a *fait accompli*. Gender roles are rangier and seem to be more permeable. And, even if they in many cases look just the same as those of our parents and grandparents, there is a major transforming difference: Today women actively choose the role, today men actively choose the role, and that makes all the difference.

Governing

Capital and *gift* are interior economies. Each offers a distinct mode of seeing the world, as well as value set, mission, and method of accounting that suffuse all manner of personal dealings and decision making. In terms of marriage, one or the other will define the living spirit of the partnership. It is an either/or proposition. Either capital *or* gift will rule. In the course of this essay I put forward the notion that the gift is the befitting economy for those couples who aspire to forge a partnership that integrates love, money, relationship, and economy.

At this point it might be fair to ask: Are there really marriages that—conscious or unconsciously—are solely founded on the capital view? Partnerships that look more like business deals? Actually, I think there are a few out there. Do they represent the majority? No, I don't think so, but perhaps this was true in the days of yore. Nevertheless, in the course of our life we do bump into this phenomenon. Been to any weddings lately? Consider the following.

Nowadays the wedding ceremony is culturally regarded as one of the most cheerful and expansive expressions of the gift. Everyone dresses to the nines. The couple exchanges vows. Gifts of crystal and porcelain and whatnot come from all quarters. Libations flow. Music and song ring out. Family and friends offer every best wish via eloquent and bombastic toasts. They bear witness to the commitment and the goodness present. In this way the whole celebration serves to bless the union of bride and groom, and the coming together of two familial streams. It is a glorious event. Bursting throughout are bright momentary smiles and glances and smooches between bride and groom, the significance of which is lost on no one: The couple is madly in love. Some might even call these small displays the best part of the wedding.

But gossip will blare if bride and groom underwhelm in the affinity and affection department, particularly if it is apparent to most that the couple is embarking on what can only be called a capital arrangement. *He just bought himself a beautiful bride. She's in it for the money. Am I right?* Or, *She's loaded. Her family's loaded. He'll make a fine kept man.* This is not mere cynicism. There's wisdom in the murmurs of the chorus. The gossip is not simply an attack on social deviance. Academic research[5] points to the likelihood that couples who primarily marry for economic security (call that capital) but not love (part and parcel of the gift) are at high risk of divorce down the road. Evidently, the idea that our financially secure couple will "learn to love each other" is false. Lack of genuine affection catches up with and plays a large part in the dissolution of many a marriage.

Although not reflective of our most enlightened side, it cannot be denied that the purely capital contract does have its appeal to the imagination—*I'll never have to worry about money again!* For some folks that part of the proposition sounds like emotional milk and honey, eternally flowing. *The security and status that I get by marrying Buster—that's love too, isn't it!* Perhaps. Except there is the not so fine print: You may find yourself in constant contact with someone eccentric, unsuitable, if not a total emotional stranger, and he will of course expect something dear in return. The considerably more troubling version of this story happens all the time: One person thinks they're coming together because of love, while the other person is there to further personal social and professional ambitions. To state the obvious in as few words as possible: This bodes ill.

. . . .

The gift is the rightful governing economy where there is ample love in relationships. Still, this doesn't mean day-to-day we reject the critical importance of selfhood and individual agendas amid marriage and family. Nor need we reject all aspects of the capital approach. Indeed, the latter is a point I'd like to elaborate on now. The capital/gift polarity finds numerous expressions beneath the victory banner of the gift economy. Life is full of capital requirements, because love doesn't pay the bills. Sometimes we do need to let the people we love fend for themselves. This is situational. At a broader level, how much capital and how much gift should a particular partnership pursue? As many of us know firsthand, striking the right balance between activities that drive financial return and activities that drive relationship return is far from easy. This is directional.

SITUATIONAL

Let's assume we embrace to the very core of our being the spirit of the gift and the Kula of Marriage. Even so, specific situations may call for a capital approach. For example, your Firstborn wants a Vespa and he's pretty clear he wants you to buy it for him. You and your spouse talk it over. On the one hand, it's just a Vespa for zipping to school and round town. On the other, it's a financial dealing that has to synchronize with your budget, your values, and what you want to transmit to Firstborn. After some deliberation, you and your spouse decide Firstborn can get a job and buy it himself. Yes, you still love him. No, you're not forking over the money. You could. But it's his moment to make it happen. If it's truly important to him, chances are very good he'll make it happen. You want him to learn this decidedly capital lesson: Adult life will be rife with capital requirements. This is an instance when you underscore that very point.

On the most immediate and practical level, the capital approach is about financially getting ahead and staying ahead. It is about covering your nut, and generating more and extra. Extra money, more options for lifestyle, greater self-reliance, and more importance and influence in the social spheres we inhabit. I intend no snarkiness here. In many ways it is true in life that we are fundamentally alone and on our own. In many ways it is imperative that we be vigilant in looking out for our own interests. Saving for a rainy day is not just some Ben Franklin goody-goody aphorism. The net of social security might not be there when it's our turn. At any moment our good job could evaporate, moreover. The last decade might have been great for making dough, but the next decade could be a dud. It's certainly happened before, and it's certainly happened to folks who were living the good life and never thought it could happen to them. So I have a real sense of respect for the way money works on the capital side of things.

The key word remains: Situational. When the capital approach is indiscriminately applied to each and every situation, then we have something else entirely. Now we are in the presence of the hero of the unsubtle, iconic book, *The Millionaire Next Door*. Capital rules. Capital governs all dealings. This is to say, you have your goals (right town, neighborhood, schools, house; right car, wardrobe; right vacations, toys; ample savings, investments, net worth) and you go for them. Either you achieve them or you don't. The determined hero of *The Millionaire Next Door* might be accused of this fundamentalism, yet not take offense in the slightest. On the contrary, he'd be proud of his convictions. *It's every man for himself out there. The sooner people get this, the better. To pay for your kid to go to college is to do that kid a great disservice! If Rupert Jr. wants to go to college, then he'll just have to pay his way. Giving him a free ride will make him soft. It will teach him success is served on a silver platter, and that's the wrong life lesson.*

The *Millionaire Next Door* (MND) protagonist is sincere, consistent, and predictable in applying his values-driven philosophy of rugged individualism. In family dealings Mr. MND will most often stick to his principles (i.e., the *capital* principles) and simply shunt aside the personal and emotional elements of the discourse. For him, it is *just business* in the family setting. *Hey, I love 'em, but money is money.* Although no doubt genuine, this modus operandi may well go hand in glove with the habit of being tight with his funds. Or, quite apart from that, it could be reflective of his distrust of the gift economy. For, the hero of *The Millionaire Next Door* does believe that gifts—what he might label "hand-outs" or "charity"—harm character. To his way of thinking, helping others too often encourages dependencies. At its worst it gives rise to entitlement in others. And Mr. MND deplores entitlement. Nothing is more appalling to him than people wanting it all *and* expecting that it be given to them. The capital economy is what he knows and trusts. It will serve as his moral compass in family money dealings, for better and for worse.

In vivid contrast stands the gift economy. As it is a considerably freer form, there is no problem with its embracing some of the wisdom of the capital approach while at the same time not being ruled by it. For instance, the use of capital *tools* in specific family dealings can make a lot of sense. These analytical tools bring an enhanced level of discipline and rigor to plans under consideration. Investing in your daughter and son-in-law's food truck, for instance, should not be an indiscriminant handout. Rather, a real business plan should be written and real due diligence performed. This doesn't make you cold or uncaring. Nor does this scare away the spirit of the gift. *Au contraire.* Reality is, you'd never ordinarily entertain the idea of such an investment, except people you love are involved and trying to find their way in the wiles of commerce. Your openness to potentially investing *in them* is reflective of the value you place on the gift economy. Relationship and connection are very important to you. Even so, that doesn't mean you have to discard the practical intelligence that capital analytics provide. Sometimes the gift economy smartly employs just such an array of capital tools.

DIRECTIONAL

In life, and at different points along the road of life, each couple must visit the matter of what mixture of power and love to strive for. In essence this is what good financial planning will periodically address, by the way. For, all couples are constantly weighing the costs and impacts of both power (governed by the capital economy) and love (governed by the gift economy). It is an existential fact of family life that some measure of both is needed. But how much of each do we choose to seek? The answer will doubtless set the life course for the relationship. Unless and until the answer—for one person or the other—changes. This, we have already seen in the case of Kevin and Holly, as well as Pablo and Betsy. Holly was ready for a life change; part of her push was based in the view that they had already earned more than enough money. Did Kevin view their family balance sheet and income statement in the same way? Don't count on it. Betsy's situation was not wholly different; the trade-off of less income by Pablo so that she could fully enroll in her MSW program seemed to her more than reasonable. Pablo had his own ideas. In the end a new meeting of the minds did in fact occur for them, which is to say, Pablo let go of his idea of taking the business to yet "another" level.

Striking the right balance between capital and gift, between power and love, between ego and partnership—is clearly values-driven. Values dictate direction. My own mix of priorities places a bit more weight toward the agendas of love, relationship, and thus the gift over the capital agendas of making money and career. That's who I am. That's what I choose. Now don't get me wrong. I like making money. I thoroughly enjoy the experiences and things that money can buy. I love my life's work, moreover, and take real pride in it. But I also cherish the emotional refuge of family, the creative spirit of relationship, and, like my parents, I will do pretty much anything for the children. In my bones I believe life is about living in the moment, but equally (to me) it's about the future, preparing and supporting the children to be its stewards. Luckily, at the present time this harmonizes with the values of my wife, Maria.

Now all that said, Maria and I have at times become so kid-centric that our own financial advisor has had to speak plainly to us about it: *Hey, the kids are in good schools and they're basically fine for the time being. Say NO to the plea for a new car. Say YES they need to work this summer for pocket money when they go back to school. Right now, you need to focus on your goals. Keep saving for retirement. Be sure to plan a fun holiday for just the two of you. Revisit the outbuilding project you've been putting off.* Indeed, our advisor was absolutely right to bring us back into balance—to not overdo offerings of the gift at the potential expense of life's capital requirements. Old age awaits us all. If we fail to put away funds for that time, then it could get weird. *Hi, kids. Can we borrow 10 bucks for Bingo Night?* This is an irony we can all live without.

In sum, the fundamental task for any couple-in-love is to strike the right balance between capital and gift AND change with the demands of the times. Balance, when we are *in the tunnel* of caring for young children, means something quite different from balance when the children are teenagers (and we can luxuriously finish an adult conversation without interruption—sort of). The meaning of balance gets morphed in countless other ways by the world: someone in our family is unwell; a career is in need of launching or, as many of us know, re-launching; perhaps a partner is retiring in her role as Vastly Overqualified Attendant of the Kitchen Sink—okay, let's say someone needs to dramatically change it up in the kitchen sink, like Betsy did; or, we ourselves are confronted with a health scare; and so on. I'm not trying to write a *Book of Changes.* More, it's the reminder that success in the Kula depends on our being deeply creative (as well as disciplined) each step of the way.

. . . .

I have spoken in praise of smartly taking care of the capital requirements of life and love. I have also praised the tools and methods and lessons of the capital approach. But *capital* in the overarching sense, in the life-guiding sense, where it functions as THE governing economy in the marriage and family—about that, I have my strong doubts. Always asserting that money is money and love is love and ne'er the twain shall meet seems dangerously facile. It might make intellectual sense, but emotionally, it makes no sense at all. The same is true for those always pursuing career ambitions and material wealth at the potential expense of relationship. Clearly it happens, and may for periods of time be required. But if capital pursuits remain the long-term driver, I can only hope—in the strangest sort of way—that love really isn't that important for such a couple. Out in the world of business, the capital approach makes obvious sense. But in home life, IF there is love, then I believe it wise to impute that heart connection into the financial and practical give-and-take of marriage *as a matter of course.* Otherwise, money will surely alienate.

Chapter 13 Treasure

Earlier, I noted that Grandma Millie and Grandpa Bill's marriage was ultimately no Kula. The problem: Bill and Millie were not equals. A level playing field is a fundamental and necessary condition for the Kula to exist. Think about it. Gift exchange between oppressed and oppressor, between haves and have-nots, between those with many options and those with few, is highly problematic. Now, it is conceivable that Grandpa could have from time to time dropped the one-up position endowed by society upon men. I'm sure that behind closed doors there were men who did just that. They felt so much love, affection, and respect for their bride that—when it really counted—they brought the power equation into relative balance. Sadly, Grandpa was not one of them.

Perhaps he cast the shadow of the Hemingway man—basically incapable of coming to terms with any sort of vulnerability in himself. But that is mere speculation. What I do know is he loved doing business the world over. Whether in India during the Second World War or occupied Japan after, he wanted his family with him, too. Grandma rolled with that for a time. They made money. They had fun. They were a good team in the good times. And then came the trying times. Grandma grew weary of being a world traveler. She hit her limit, and wished to go home once and for all. Besides, they had finally made good money, more than they ever imagined. It was at this point that their individual agendas diverged, and the power inequity in the relationship reared its ugly head.

Grandpa would not yield.

I don't know why. Perhaps Grandpa got drunk on success. The allure of making good money and being important has brought down greater men than he. Or, perhaps success sharpened his appetite for greater achievement. *Enough is not enough. I'm just getting started!* To be fair, these are subtle and shifting career lines for anyone to figure out. It was true then. It is true now. Look at the thriving business of life and career coaching; many of us seek the counsel of others just so we don't lose perspective, so we don't wreak havoc on those who are near and dear to us. Whatever the reason, Grandpa had no intention of leaving occupied Japan. *The world is my home,* he declared. Not another word was spoken on this major life decision.

With the passage of time Grandma recognized the futility of overtly pursuing the issue. And although she dutifully served Grandpa, it was thenceforward devoid of sweetness and affection. This was Grandma's passive-aggressive equivalent of throwing china at her esteemed husband. Right or wrong, it was a wake-up call delivered in the only way she knew how. She withdrew her love.

At first, Grandpa did not see what was going on. But when he did, a number of us in the family believe it pierced his armor and badly wounded him. The notion that he might have had some part to play in all this, much less that he'd been ever high-handed, was lost on him. I infer this, of course, from how badly he responded. Indeed, he ordered Grandma to take the girls, teenagers at this point, and return stateside. They went. But his fury remained. It consumed him and he went to a very dark place. Instead of trying to pick up the pieces, instead of even superficially trying to understand how frustrated Grandma felt, he became vindictive. Two years later he returned from Japan, accompanied by a woman who would, for the next 30 years, never again overtly challenge his authority. That woman was Fumiko. Grandma was out. Forever.

Some years later—like ten—Grandma moved in with Mom, Dad, and us rowdy kids. No one ever informed us Grandma was suffering from a broken heart, though we all knew something was up as my cousin's summer-of-'68 wedding approached. That wedding would have Bill, Millie, and Fumiko in the same room for the first and last time. Understandably, it had put Grandma in a whole summer's worth of funks. Then came the wedding day. All gathered at our house before going to the church. Few words were spoken. There was almost no eye contact. But the vibe in the room was bad. Zeus and Hera in a black mood would have had nothing on Bill and Millie.

Grandma never tried romance again. Perhaps this made her The Vanquished. Then again she emerged from this misfortune in a way that no one could have foreseen. She became the indispensable right hand "man" in the business successes of first, my father, and then, my mother. Grandma had game! Twenty more years of it, in fact.

Still, I can't help but wonder what could have been. I recall a number of years ago an older cousin saying to me, *I think what Millie needed was an assertiveness training course.* Perhaps the gumption Clementine Churchill displayed might have helped, though it's so hard to say. Yielding was a clear sign of weakness to Grandpa. But *never* yielding—Grandpa failed to consider the cost of absolute rule. If depth of hurt is an indicator of depth of love, then Grandma and Grandpa once had great affection between them. But amid prosperity, they somehow lost it all.

AFTER BITTER, SWEET

In his six-plus decades of political life, Winston Churchill was both iconic and iconoclastic. He was the rarest of political animals, consistently (and eloquently) infuriating friend and foe alike. Churchill's friends lambasted him for atrocious lapses in political judgment. His enemies repeatedly attacked him as egomaniacal. There was accuracy on both accounts. At times Churchill was wildly full of himself. At times he did dangerously lack the most basic instinct of politics: Self-preservation. Enamored of what Victorian England and the Empire had once been, Churchill never wavered in his love of the crown; but when, amid the monarchical crisis of 1938, he lectured Parliament and country on unconditional loyalty to the crown, it was received very badly. So badly, in fact, that many of Churchill's most ardent admirers thought he was a goner this time.

Even Churchill thought he was done for. Having been on the verge of political extinction several times before, he had had allies then. By "allies" I don't mean friends; rather, relationships of expedience, bound by history, and flying (for the most part) under the banner of the Tory conservative party. But now, Churchill's fiercely independent style had caught up with him. In terms of toeing the Tory party line, no one had been more irreverent than Sir Winston. Then came the payback. For much of the 1930's the Tory conservatives, who held power, relegated him to the backbench of Parliament, shrewdly yet idiotically muting his voice at the very time when, with Nazi Germany rising, Churchill's leadership was needed most.

What brought Churchill back from his political near-death experience, of course, was that he was right. Since 1933, his repeated warnings of the fascist rise in Germany, far from being histrionic or self-serving, were spot on. The same was true of his gadfly politics. Churchill continually poked at British complacency and naïveté in an era when people pined for peace. Meantime, the world was in a hell of a state, the ruling Tories knew it, but they lacked the courage of candor. They failed to speak candidly to king or people. It was not until Austria was annexed, Czechoslovakia overrun, and Poland hours from defeat, that His Majesty's government declared war against the Nazis. Vindicated and now in demand, Churchill was forthwith made First Lord of the Admiralty, a position he occupied in the First World War.

But Britain was woefully ill-prepared for war. The German military and business sector had been productive, efficient, and one pointed in their seven years of preparation, *while*—as Churchill famously penned it—*England slept*. Fortunately, Britain had Churchill. It was to him they would turn in Britain's darkest hour. It was to him they would listen on the wireless (aka radio), because he had the gift of oratory, a gift that roused the spirit of this great, though at that moment, frightened nation. Churchill, this remarkably resilient lord, now Prime Minister of a 1,000-year-old nation on the verge of extinction, represented their final hope. As we well know, he would not let them down.

But life certainly is full of curious twists and turns. Five years later, after Churchill and the Allies turned the tide and delivered victory, what sort of victory parade would be waiting for Sir Winston? By Jove, he promptly got voted out of office! Apparently, the country that loved him in times of war wanted nothing to do with him in times of peace. Not this 1945 peace anyway. Dizzyingly, the British people would change their mind again in a few years' time, making him prime minister for a second time.

Given all this, given Churchill's very public record as brilliant leader who was often provocative and always evocative, the question naturally arises: How could he have been such a sweetie in marriage? How could he have been half, albeit the lesser half, of what might be regarded as one of the great marriages of the 20th century?

In a word, Sir Winston chose the Kula. He trusted his instincts, and apropos marriage, his instincts were right. He traded in a little power, and got the riches of the gift in turn. This stands out. Nothing normative pushed him this way. Of course, Churchill wasn't pushed by norms in any quarter of his life. Here, though, it clearly worked. He chose the Kula in the beginning, in the middle, and in the end. History shows that it paid dividends for both him and Clemmie.

The Kula was the organizing principle of their partnership. Doubtless there were times when each forgot the Kula, but then returned. This is what we encountered at the outset of *Lion Hearted Love.* Winston was being obtuse, definitely not his best self; and Clemmie responded in wrathful fashion. Immediately, Winston got the message, acknowledged his folly, remembered the Kula, and set things right. It was Clemmie's time to live a piece of her dream. Their love would return anew. How do we know? The following correspondence was one of hundreds. This particular one took place not long after Clemmie set sail on her big adventure. On New Year's Day she wrote from Madras:

"Oh my Darling, I'm thinking so much of you & how you have enriched my life. I have loved you very much but I wish I had been a more amusing wife to you. How nice it would be if we were young again."

He replied that she had written "some words vy dear to me about my having enriched yr life. I cannot tell you what pleasure this gave me, because I always feel so overwhelmingly in yr debt, if there be accounts in love. It was sweet of you to write this to me, & I hope & pray I shall be able to make you happy & secure during my remaining years, and cherish you my darling one as you deserve, & leave you in comfort when my race is run. What it has been to me to live all these years in yr heart & companionship no phrases can convey. Time passes swiftly, but is it not joyous to see how great and growing is the treasure we have gathered together, amid the storms & stresses of so many eventful & to millions tragic & terrible years?"[6]

. . . .

This is the sweetness of partnership. To really enjoy and value each other's company, whether the fires of passion burn bright or gently warm—this is friendship, this is what makes the relationship continually evolve. Winston yielded in his marriage. Clemmie, for her part, rose to the occasion. Theirs was a great union. They ever kept the gift moving and alive. Indeed, their lifelong partnership became, as Winston so elegantly wrote, this great and growing treasure ... a little broken china notwithstanding.

Mid-Amble

The opening essay of *Lion Hearted Love* concerned itself with the marital partnership. What's really going on? How might we regard the give-and-take? How do we strike a balance between the capital and gift agendas? Ultimately, we'd like money and economy to reinforce and support the wealth of the relationship. Now it's time to change it up. The aim is less about wisdom and the arcs of life and much more about the day-to-day, practical side of doing personal money. *We'd like to do personal money exceedingly well.* I mean nothing poetic by that statement. How effectively we spend and save is mission-critical. Same can be said for planning & implementing, investing, and overall financial decision making. We'd like to configure the marital partnership to be its most potent.

You might think after marital partners harmonize on the Kula level that figuring out how best to save, spend, plan, invest, etc. (and who does what) would naturally fall into place. It doesn't. For, the journey itself seems to be characterized by Odyssean obstacles and challenges. This needn't dampen our spirits. On the contrary, I think there is great cheer in familiarizing ourselves with the predictable (and predictably unpredictable) dynamics at play, with getting our expectations in line, and meeting life's money challenges with the acuity and deftness of Odysseus. Indeed, the Homeric hero is often referred to as the Great Tactician, and for good reason: The guy knew how to solve nettlesome problems, one after the other, and bring all riches back home! Metaphorically, we can manifest in similar fashion, even if we don't record it in epic form.

No doubt, the fun side of money and wealth and having extra is just that—fun. Then we can allocate resources to bring together family and friends, to feast well into the night, to enjoy creature comforts and cool toys, to be enriched by diverse educational experiences, to gain the perspective of travel, to take inspiration from objects of beauty, to feel the smile of enhanced social status, and to know the heartfelt goodness of generosity and being able to support and assist family and friends. This is but a short list, of course. And while it's true there exists a raft of individuals who psychologically struggle to relax with their good fortune (we'll meet these characters soon enough), most of us really need no education on how to enjoy this peak side of money.

At the same time, no one's money life is all smooth sailing. No one's money life is forever peril-free. It is common knowledge that money issues are at the epicenter of marital conflicts, alongside disagreements about housework and other domestic-centric responsibilities, aka the kitchen sink. Part of the issue is that money-in-marriage is not a go-with-the-flow proposition. Because we have an otherwise very good and loving and supportive relationship with our spouse, we might naturally assume that such harmony extends to how we work together around money. But in the majority of cases we'd be mistaken. This is provocative, not just for what it says about us humans, but for what it also says about money's alchemical nature. In pith: *Personal money activates highly charged and deeply rooted differences in many couples.* This may not seem like much of an insight, but as will be shown, this ordinary truth has far-reaching and chaotic effects. It also explains, in part, why personal money is intrinsically and predictably tricky, if not thorny for couples.

To serve as placeholder, consider the following illustration that will only make sense if we can agree on the following premise: Some people are horrid at handling certain aspects of their personal money world. Can we agree on this? I don't want to get into the issue of pathology or whether such people can be fixed, only get agreement on the real-time truth of the premise, which I think is reasonable: Some people are awful at handling some or all facets of their personal finances. Now let's take the next step: What if such a person were primary manager of family finances, yet not aware he's quite horrid at it?

In case you need convincing that it does happen, consider (for now) the incident involving our beloved and mercurial Sir Winston, controller of the Churchill family purse. The time was the late 1930's and Winston was "suddenly" very concerned about money. Clearly this was not the first time, nor would it be the last that he'd be seized with sudden fear about personal finances. So, Randolph and Sarah (adult children) were summoned to the Churchill's country home, Chartwell. Their allowance would be tightened forthwith. Clemmie, too, knew the drill; time to tighten up, though she already was frugal. As for the main culprit, the one who usually felt no financial stress at all, who habitually tore through precious savings and lived light years beyond the family's means—well, suffice to say that Winston failed to put *that party* on notice.

Par for the course: Financial problems were consistently

difficult if not impossible to solve because Winston failed the First Step—to gain a clear and accurate picture of himself, of his strengths and weaknesses in the personal finance domain. Now we might say that Winston was an extreme case, and that would most definitely be true, but isn't it also true that the personal money world is bursting with characters behaving and emoting in the extreme? More, such characters almost always regard their ways and means as, well, perfectly normal, yes? But let's take this inquiry down by a few degrees of intensity. That brings into focus those who are not particularly extreme, but who most certainly underwhelm and underperform, leaving themselves vulnerable to experiencing the long fall to financial mediocrity. How does the long fall come about? What keeps us from seeing it in our self or our partner? It's a topic we'll be sure to take up.

On a personal and qualitative level, I should note that suffused throughout the assertions, speculations, and think pieces in the second half of this book is one undeniably Shambhalian[7] invitation—*the invitation to rouse fearlessness in our mind and heart.* By this I mean we are willing to cut through biases, self-concepts, and other assumptions that make us feel comfortable (and powerful) in our world, but which too often work against us. Being effective and skillful like Odysseus is impossible if we can't get out of our own way. The problems and challenges that inevitably and periodically arise are hard enough to solve in the best of circumstances. Accordingly, we'd like to recognize and every day create the best of circumstances. We do that in other parts of our life. Why not here?

In the warrior tradition of Shambhala, *fearlessness* is inseparable from the willingness to be who we are, without any sort of self-aggression (or self-deception, for that matter). We relax our idea of who we wish we were. This is an important point. Who we want to be and who we in fact are don't always jibe. Relationship, perhaps like no other vehicle in life, has a way of pointing this out, care of the one we dearly love. Dropping this big inner investment in our self-concept, even relaxing it, takes tremendous openness and courage: Lion-heartedness. But the payoff is direct. Compelling. We become freshly curious about who we are and what's going on in the phenomenal world, as opposed to assuming that it's all good. Sometimes, it's NOT all good. Sometimes, discernments must be made. Insights must be gained.

In the business world this approach defines the emerging HR (human resources) practice now. I am just returning from a Moss-Adams consultancy conference to help wealth managers get better at running their businesses more like, um, businesses— a common problem in my line of work. More than an hour of the morning's discussion was devoted to hiring and managing staff. The title of the discussion was "Leveraging Human Capital." Time and time again a panel of very successful execs in the industry asserted these two messages: 1) Put people in positions that energize them, and 2) Have them do psychological testing, the intent being that they, you, and everyone in the company know what their strengths and weaknesses are. Everyone should know everyone's strengths, weaknesses, and styles. I call this the Open Book model for partnerships and teams. It's clearly potent. It also takes the personal sting out of misunderstandings, because it starts with the notion that differences *naturally* make for complication in communication. Differences take time to identify and reconcile. They have to be worked through. I love this ethos.

There are three essays to come. The first tackles control and responsibility in regards to the purse. Commingle funds, or no? Why? What are some of the real-life variables at play? How to orient? In the second essay we take up the aforementioned broader theme: How can we organize our financial world so that it plays to the strengths of each person? It's one of those simple HR concepts that can prove elusive-in-action. Without it, certain financial checks and balances might get neglected. Decisions might get made in haphazard fashion. And worst of all: Lessons might get lost, or altogether forgotten. The marital partnership will surely leak—leak money, at the very least. The third and final essay ruminates on the brass tacks of money. We can reject working a budget, for example, but in so doing, positive outcomes become exceedingly more difficult to achieve. Or, we can have all sorts of expectations about what prosperity *should* mean for us, but when it arrives, some darned good financial planning had best be ready to harness what in fact are energetic and exciting winds—or else those winds are sure to blow us all over the place. Prosperity is rife with ironies. They weren't lost on Odysseus. They won't be lost on us.

ESSAY

II

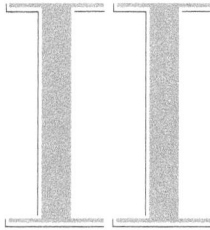

PURSE
MUSINGS

Chapter 14 Control and the Purse

There is much debate about it right now, and rightly so. Should couples have separate finances, commingled, or some hybrid of the two? What are the pivotal factors? The traditional arrangement of one joint checking account still gets a lot of action. The modern iteration of separate purses also has its loyal and growing following. I don't think there is one categorical answer to espouse here. Rather, there are situational specifics (i.e., inheritance) and relationship factors (stable, unstable) that shape what's going on. Inherited money is fundamentally and karmically different. Money in an unstable relationship obviously must be handled in line with the possibility of break-up, whereas money in a stable relationship affords considerable leeway. Thus, my objective is to orient, to point out what I (and other veteran advisors) regard as basic rules of thumb, and within that to encourage each person to figure out what arrangement feels appropriate.

This purse and control stuff has a way of becoming very touchy. Dilemmas also lurk. Doing what is "by the book" can be fraught with relationship complication, sometimes lifelong complication. Ditching what is "by the book" can also be dangerous.

What to do? *I love him, but for a number of reasons I know it's right to keep these monies separate. They're not marital assets; they're my assets, given to me by my parents. Hubby is a little miffed about it, even after all these years. Sometimes he throws it in my face in the middle of an argument. Jeez, Louise!* At the present time I have no solution for this kind of money-in-relationship discord; nor have I—as of this writing—heard a therapist prescribe the relationship cure for it. No one should have to share control for the good of the relationship, but, quite understandably, many a spouse will be less than understanding about that decision. Here, money figures in like a wild and intractable character. More to come on this.

As to the more tamable side in matters of purse management and control, I believe the issue is more one of checks and balances than arguing about which model is better—i.e., one purse (theirs) v. three purses (his, hers, theirs). The One Purse model is highly effective because—in its mature form—it leverages the diverse strengths of each person. Dividing and delegating tasks makes it efficient. And, done well, the One Purse model constantly reaffirms the notion of partnership: one P&L, one income statement, one partnership, and (not to go Bob Marley on you) one love. The One Purse model is a terrible idea, however, if the relationship is unstable or, worse, the person in control is less than impeccable. I won't address the latter for obvious reasons *(um, get out of there yesterday!)*, but regarding relationship instability, the Three Purse model makes a lot of sense. It lets you have the means to execute a ready-made exit plan just in case.

Checks and balances is serious stuff. Pardon the bossiness, but: You and your partner really do have to have state-of-the-partnership meetings with some regularity, at least two or three per year. Agenda items: How are the budget-to-actual numbers faring? Are there big expenses or savings goals on the horizon?

What's changed in the past six months? What do we have and where is it? How are our investments performing? Is the risk profile right on them? The formatting of such reports takes time. Obviously, financial planners and advisors can be helpful not only with the gathering and formatting of the information, but with "holding the space," as they say, so the two of you can discuss the critical issues in a direct yet kind manner.

Checks and balances does not, however, mean you have to be involved in every single decision. Nor does it mean you handle the nuts and bolts of bill pay or haggling with the car salesman (you may do some, or next to none). BUT, it does mean you periodically engage. You tune into the medium-to-very-big decisions, get the key information, and make your voice heard. To not engage is foolish. I mean that. I recently spoke with a gentleman here in town whom everybody likes—I believe the word is simpatico—well, he has simpatico. Our conversation veered onto money and marriage, and at one point he said quite seriously to me: *I don't tell my wife anything. She rides her horses at the barn and that's all she needs to know.* I was shocked! Thought this was the worst of 1950's all over again. More: What about this guy's wife? Where was her head at?

Trust is what makes the ecosystem of the purse work. It can't run without it. But a word on what Trust is not: It's not foregoing checks and balances. *What? You don't trust me? Go back to bed. I got it all under control!* is not trust. Be formal in your marital money dealings, and, yes, be very careful about making assumptions. We change our mind sometimes, and our partner does too. Maybe she's no longer as keen on buying that car, house, or making that investment as she once was. Maybe she wants to keep those funds in saving so you or she can carry a lighter workload. Sometimes a life event—death of parent, health scare, spiritual crisis—changes what's abiding deep in your heart. These changes will act alchemically upon your money. And as to being formal in matters of money-in-relationship, I suggest you develop your own ritual to slow things down, to ensure that you both engage; to be sure you gather the latest info, hold the key conversations, evaluate the "operations," and in a kind and direct way hold each other accountable. This may well be the best antidote to half-baked plans and hack decisions that can otherwise proliferate when your partner (or you) unilaterally takes the helm.

Chapter 15 Dilemma of Separate Finances

B efore moving to Boulder a few years back, Todd and Trina both worked serious corporate jobs in the DC area and from the look of it did very well for themselves. At least well enough to build from scratch the very sweet and sweeping Georgian house up the street from us. As luck would have it, our dinner date with them coincided with the recent launch of Trina's new business. Without going into it, I loved her business concept and it was clear that she was six or seven thousand hours into developing the concept and turning it into a real business. The initial response from the marketplace, in terms of sales, was quite good. But Trina was dissatisfied, a bit melancholic, and definitely stressed. It was odd. It was as if she wanted it to be successful FASTER! Though as any entrepreneur worth her salt knows, businesses grow as they grow and it's often times not in your control, no matter how hard you work or how brilliant the concept. Things take time. Still, Trina was pressing and it wasn't at all clear why.

The subject of money visited the dinner table throughout the evening. At some point Todd and Trina shared thoughts on how and why they employed the Three Purse system of *his, hers, and theirs.* It was a topic about which Trina was particularly impassioned. Not ending up economically dependent like her mom had been a goal of Trina's for as long as she can remember. Being her own person, having her own career, was another life goal with equally deep roots. It hasn't been easy for women. Still isn't. Symbolic of her independence, her professional accomplishments, and to a degree her self-esteem—the money in her separate bank account was clearly no ordinary currency. Her words were heartfelt. Of course, economically and legally she still wasn't as independent and mobile as she thought. For what is earned during the marriage—regardless of by whom—is in almost all cases regarded as marital property: Each party effectively owns half of the savings, investments, and the appreciation on those assets that take place during the marriage. Obviously, the psychological symbolism of the Three Purse system was not lost on Todd, who conveyed the nonverbal attitude of: *Why get in the way of something that clearly makes my partner happy?*

As to nuts and bolts of the Three Purse system, Todd and Trina had worked them diligently for years, each contributing to shared expenses, each contributing to holidays and special gifts, and so on. Listening to them, I appreciated how engaged each had to have been every step of the way. Not for everyone, I know. But it sounded like it really worked for them. Until the awkward moment unexpectedly arrived, ushered in by an off-the-cuff remark from Trina. Suddenly looking a bit wistful, she said that retirement was approaching, and there was this not so small hitch: She had put away a whole lot less than Todd for that shared goal of retirement fun in the sun. The details of her shortfall were not clear and I certainly did not inquire, though my guess is that it was substantial. What happened? I could only guess Trina had made—here and there—lifestyle decisions that diminished her earnings and savings power, perhaps to spend more time with their daughter, perhaps to pursue her passion for interior design. Whatever the cause, it was now clear what lay beneath her impatience with her recent business launch. As for Todd, he was inscrutably silent.

. . . .

How this will unfold over time is far from clear. I doubt Todd is simply a cold S.O.B. who—in all cases—will enjoy the afternoon of his life reading espionage thrillers at the beach while Trina toils away in pursuit of the missing gold. But right now it does seem like his message to her is: *Honey, I love ya, but yes, you do need to go out there and make some more money. Fair is fair.* In this Separate Purse scenario, what happens if Trina doesn't meet with earnings success over the next decade? At retirement, will she get bailed out by Todd, or somewhat bailed out, or will they need to sell their big house, or live less adventurously? To reiterate, I believe Todd truly loves Trina, but what will the emotional toll be in a disparity scenario? How aggrieved will Todd feel if he ends up carrying more of the financial weight and enjoying fewer life adventures because Trina did not fulfill her end of the bargain? How will Trina feel about Todd's negativity? Or: Maybe the shortfall won't matter. Maybe there will be room for the spirit of the gift in the eleventh hour, and Todd says, *Don't worry about it, Trina. You gave it your best effort.* All purse management scenarios have risks. This one is no exception. What started out as a nice, clean plan could still lead to a money-in-relationship mess. We shall see, of course.

Chapter 16 Legacy

A spouse's Separate Purse holds a central place in matters of inheritance. Inherited money *is* different. Among veteran wealth advisors, I believe the following is normative: *Inheritance is regarded as a spouse's separate property. Integrating it into the marital picture may or may not be appropriate. No one violates the letter or spirit of the relationship by keeping inherited assets apart from the family purse.* This view, of course, has rubbed more than a few non-inheriting spouses the wrong way. That is too bad. Of the many exceptional situations that arise in matters of money-in-relationship, this is definitely one. Inheritance is simply not marital property—not legally, not energetically—and as such the responsibility for it falls to him/her who receives it. That includes control, of course. The person who inherits is necessarily the one in control of these monies. Will he/she be up to the task? We all hope so. From time to time, however, an otherwise mature adult does go on a spender bender with the inheritance, leaving his partner feeling helpless and furious. One such a story is right around the corner.

Inherited money teems with karma. It is the money of strong

ties. People do not (as a rule) bestow the fruits of their labors upon casual acquaintances or strangers. Even in regards to good friends, people seldom choose to leave money to them over, say, their children. As to the matter of sons- and daughters-in-law, I readily recognize that the quality of harmonious and respectful connection is all over the map. But even in the best of circumstances, when the older generation loves their daughter's husband "like a son," they're still most likely to leave the inheritance solely to their daughter. This is no slap in the face to beloved son-in-law. It's practical. It's age-old. There's nothing wrong with recognizing the strongest tie at play—the one they have with their daughter. Not coincidentally, the matter of legacy also figures in here.

The word *legacy* at its root connotes stewardship. Inheritance is surely your asset to do with as you please, but most likely you will also feel a certain responsibility to fulfill some or all of the grantor's wishes, be they implied or overt. This issue of stewardship and obligation to the grantor is incredibly complicated, as well as varied and personal. I do think it's fine that one passes along one's material wealth to another with certain expectations, although obviously those expectations will run the gamut: from supportive, affirming, visionary, and well-wishing to distracting, guilt-riddling, manipulative, and oppressive. Taming the emotional legacy that oftentimes accompanies the financial legacy is a topic about which the family therapy community, I suspect, has much to say. While an important line of inquiry, it is not the one we'll follow right now.

In the fore is the issue of control. He/she who inherits is the rightful controller. But what about when said inheritance falls into the hands of one who is immature, unreliable, and unprepared? Will the wife, say, have to suffer her fool husband? I'm afraid so. Obviously, she can beg, plead, and try all manner of persuasion on him, but in the end it's his to squander or to steward. He may recognize his shortcomings, his propensity to have the cash burn a hole in his pocket, his lack of investor focus or acumen, and thus be open to counsel and assistance. Great! Then again he may not, thereby snatching defeat from the jaws of victory and good fortune.

Not long after the publication of my first book *(Zen Money Blues)* I received a detailed email correspondence from a friend of a friend, a woman in her late 60's who lived in San Francisco, where she had raised three children and some fifteen years prior had divorced her husband of 25 years. Robert (her ex) had been a big-time EST trainer in town. Business was great. Still, one rarely gets rich in the self-help industry, and so, as Martha, his ex-wife, described it, *We white-knuckled our way through a modest upper middle class existence.* The annual year-end gifts from Martha's family were essentially how they made ends meet. *I took those funds before Robert could get his hands on them and paid off the horrifying credit card balance we accumulated during the year.*

Things more or less hung together financially for Robert and Martha because Financial Trouble then was harder to get into. This is to say, credit wasn't as free and easy as it would become during the late 90's and early 2000's mortgage boom. But when Robert's mother died in 1993 and he inherited a million bucks, all hell broke loose anyway. *A million dollars was a lot of money in 1993,* Martha noted. *Thank God he set aside some of that money for the children's college. Four years for Pomona, Berkeley, and Chico State. As for the rest of the money—oy! He'd always wanted tailored suits, so he flew to London and bought obscenely expensive suits on Jermyn Street.* "You only live once," *he said, and so began his sartorial spender bender. He bought a five thousand dollar leather sofa, to lie on while listening to classical music. He bought three thousand dollars worth of CDs, and he didn't even have a CD player! He fixed that, of course. Stereo equipment: The bill was huge. Even he knew it was huge because he hid the bill from me. Anyway, you get the picture. It was his money. And there was nothing I could really say or do about it. I knew he was going to blow it all, and that none of it—not a penny—was earmarked for OUR retirement. That's when I just decided to hunker down. Protect our other assets with an eye to finding the right time to leave the marriage. After my mother died, a decent sum came my way—not a ton of money, mind you, but enough for me to say, "I'll make it work. Not another day of this madness. I'm leaving this marriage once and for all."*

. . . .

Recently, Martha and I met up for tea and further discussed her plight. *Tell me: There's nothing I could have done with Robert's inheritance, right?* Right. The money simply wasn't hers or theirs. *I tried to talk sense into him, but that money was morphine. I can't blame the demise of our marriage on this crazy period, though. We had our differences, lots of 'em. Oh, Robert—he sure was obtuse when it came to his own hang-ups around money. You know, some days I almost forgive the guy.*

ESSAY

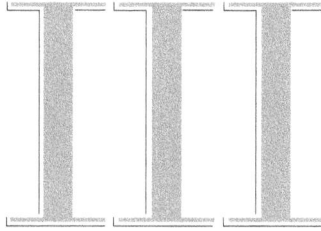

OPEN

BOOK

Chapter 17 Open Book

The daily operations level of money—as per saving & spending, planning & implementing, investing, and, not least, making critical financial decisions—presents very real challenges to the marital partnership. We'd like to turn this to our advantage *as soon as humanly possible.* Where that's not likely or possible, we at least want to actively manage the situation before it manages us. To go a little corporate on you, we'd like to Leverage Human Capital! In the truly progressive companies, we find HR people, company managers, and business owners who are quite serious about actually and consistently doing this. To wit, they're vetting personnel, as well as hiring coaches from the outside, so as to build highly effective teams. The process is quite basic: Identify the strengths and weaknesses of each player, organize the teams/departments, and assign tasks and positions accordingly. Some companies take the process to an edgy and compelling next level: Everyone on the team is made aware of everyone else's identified strengths and weaknesses. For our money-in-relationship purposes, I like this a lot. Think of it as going Open Book.

Of course, marriage is an enterprise conspicuously distinct

from business. It takes place where we eat, sleep, make love, and let down our guard. Its bottom line (mission) includes measures of both profit (capital) and love (gift). And in the marital enterprise, we live with our partner. Once we go Open Book there, once we cop to our identifiable strengths and weaknesses in regards to spending & saving, planning & implementing, investing, and the like—once we do that, it could get thrown in our face. And, this is why the ethos of Shambhala *fearlessness* is so crucial: If we have a good marriage, if we have a good relationship, then we need to take this risk, and we simultaneously need to shed the tendency of aggression toward our self and/or our partner. Otherwise there's no way to go forward, there's no way to become prodigious problem solvers in the personal money realm.

What challenges lie immediately ahead? The vividly human kind, inseparable from: pain and pleasure, affinity and opposition, behaviors in the extreme, and the natural resistance to identifying personal weaknesses. As for plot line: Love, life, and money dealings have carried many a good man and woman to financial destinations they never (for better and for worse) dreamed of. This is what happened to Paul and Elisabeth Marylebone. They went with the flow for six or seven years, and no one paid any of it a second thought. Paul was at the financial helm, all by his lonesome. This was not ideal. A lithe and clever chap with a walk akin to Cary Grant, Paul Marylebone systematically lent a little cash here to family and a little cash there to friends, and he also made a couple of horrid, speculative bets. "They weren't big, maybe thirty grand each." He referred to them as "investments," though he'd lost all his money in them. Paul also had "a liberated, unorthodox relationship to money," or so he noted during our initial phone consultation. Elisabeth herself was eerily terse on that call, though did manage to convey she only very recently realized that finances were terribly adrift under the current regime.

By the by, the predicament of the Marylebones should NOT be regarded solely as ironic. Just because Paul Marylebone is recognized in the community as a "Therapist's Therapist," a master therapist to whom those in the pickle business (aka psychotherapy) turn when they themselves feel in a pickle, does not place him beyond the reach of financial chaos and mediocrity. To be sure, the great psychotherapists of this modern world are master tacticians, Odysseus-like in their sharp perceptions of the moment and canny in identifying the unlikely ingredients for possible solutions, but sometimes it's hard for any one of us to get a good clean look at ourselves, to find that undistorted mirror to look into—to even think in the first place to do this! Of course, spouses worldwide seldom fail to mirror back to us our less than stellar qualities; but the question is: Will they do it in time? How bad will the damages be? Paul and Elisabeth, I believe, will find their way back to a healthy financial groove, but first Paul will have to get real. This I was to learn firsthand during their in-person consult.

UN-EPIC VOYAGE TO MEDIOCRITY

Boulder, Colorado (June 2008) – "You ask me how I'm doing? I gather you mean, financially speaking," Elisabeth says, and pauses not. "Well, I'm doing as people do who one day realize they're living a lie. I'm upset. Perplexed. Disappointed. Frustrated. Scared."

"We're not living a lie," Paul interrupts.

"This man is clueless about money," she cuts across, but never looks at him. "I love him, but he's driving me mad. The money fights … terrible … go nowhere. But we're not here to hash all that out. I've come prepared with numbers. By my pencil on the napkin calculation, and it is a kindly one at that, we have about 60% of the funds we should have put away for retirement. The rest of that money—just frittered away."

She arches her otherwise pleasant eyebrows at Paul.

"I'm not taking the bait," Paul says.

We have barely sat down and the atmosphere is tense. Still, I seek information about what they have, what they owe, how much money they make, and where it goes. We stick to the numbers, not stories. This tack seems to mollify. Traces of a tone of civility are discernable. But the Universe has its own ideas on this particular day and plainly rapprochement is not one of them.

Smack! Brack! Ack!

Thunk!

There is a racket on the street. It pierces the moment and demands our undivided attention. There is the clattering sound of skateboard over sidewalk and the grunt of wheels hitting ruts and cracks in the pavement. The sound carries five stories up to our conference room where fatefully the French doors are wide open. Now not that acoustics should particularly matter for a punk rock band or a clatter-grunt skateboard, but the acoustics are good. Too good.

Oh, my! Paul gasps.

Elisabeth shakes her head in disgust.

"I was not trying to rebel against you or what we had agreed on, I swear," Paul says. He looks to me as if there is something I can do. I have no idea what's going on! "I was at the mall, doing errands, and I saw this skateboard."

"This bloody $200 skateboard," she corrects, bitterly.

"Yes, that," he says. "She's making too much of this."

"It's why I called this meeting."

"I will not accept Guilty As Charged. Allow me to explain,"

Paul insists.

The skinny was this: Paul's sister and 15-year-old nephew had been visiting from Connecticut and were headed home the next day when Paul gave his nephew a $200 skateboard as a present.

"I saw it and it made me think of Kevin," Paul says. "Kevin should have this. I don't know skateboards but it struck me as a very good one. I admit I forgot to look at the price. Big deal! We all make mistakes. Besides, how many 15-year-old nephews come and visit you in Colorado?"

Elisabeth tries to keep her eye makeup from smearing and she waves Paul off as he tries to speak further.

"What is wrong with this guy?" she finally gets out. "Please tell me. Please. We've got a daughter in high school; she goes to college year after next; we've saved some but nothing like our parents did for us. Paul's cousin has mooched us silly, with some jackass deal on a sailboat on the Cape that we've used once in eight years. I'm glad we spent the time and the money to be with Paul's brother Ned when he was fighting cancer, but that was financially prohibitive—chipping in to cover the treatments and special care. His mother is house rich and cash poor after all the money spent on his dad's Alzheimer's care: Did anyone ever think of buying long-term care? Apparently not. Now we have to make sure that his mom is going to be OK. That may well fall solely to us. Paul, meantime, is burnt out on his therapy work. He needs a sabbatical. And then he looks at me and says, 'It's only money, Honey. Look at how happy that made Kevin feel. Did you see his eyes light up?' And I tell him, 'We see Kevin once every seven years. We don't have money like that. You're a fool! Don't you see how this undercuts us?'"

Elisabeth dabs at her eyes. Long gone is the sound of the skateboard.

"I'm tired and deeply confused," Paul says softly. "I've lost all perspective."

. . . .

After considerable flailing about, Paul has emotional and financial hell to pay. His journey to mediocrity comes of many small and a few mid-sized miscues, multiplied by seven years. For a man in the business of insight, it was awfully hard for him to come to terms with the truth of his financial track record. Although Paul is in the main to blame, Elisabeth certainly went along for the ride. Indeed, *What was she thinking?* Fortunately, with some key changes to personnel and some hard work, their situation still holds the possibility of redemption. First, though, let's do a brief post-consultation analysis.

In no particular order, consider the following blind spots and mental shortcuts, at times shared by both of them, that contributed to the outcome of financial mediocrity:

1) Elisabeth assumed that Paul, being an intelligent and educated man, was fully up to managing the family finances by himself. But such a rational view doesn't bear out. Research says education and intelligence augur well for earning a good income, but isn't an indicator for being a good manager of one's personal finances.[8]

2) Paul assumed that, too.

3) Elisabeth trusted Paul. Indeed, he was trustworthy *as a person*. But it did not logically follow that he'd therefore be a competent manager of their money. In terms of the partnership, we can say that she did not engage for this period of their life. In so doing, there was no accountability—no checks and balances.

4) Paul was a good earner. Therefore, he must know all he needs to about personal money. The same thing, right? Actually,

not at all. The ability to make money says little about our capacity and competencies to manage various aspects of personal finances in stellar fashion. There's no correlation.

5) Elisabeth was a good soul. Friend to many, she dedicated herself to serving family and community when not promoting her art. Accordingly, her belief was this: *Be virtuous and the rest will take care of itself.* That belief included money. The problem is, the money did not take care of itself. It fell by default to the wrong person—her husband, Paul. Not a bad sort, he nevertheless turned out to be a gent with a spotty track record, the kind that is illustrative of taking the un-epic voyage to mediocrity.

6) Did unconscious gender assumptions play in? Did Paul and Elisabeth both default to a traditional view that the man of the house is responsible for the finances? Progressive people though they are, I do wonder.

7) Reprise: Where were the checks and balances? Where was the engagement?

Chapter 18 Story of Differences

To paraphrase the great baseball player and manager, Yogi Berra—er, actually, I mean the immortal Greek philosopher, Socrates: *The unexamined financial life ain't worth trusting.* For all Paul Marylebone's professional acuity, it never dawned on him to turn that sharp penetrating professional mind on himself. Very understandable. Very human. But freshly bruised from the fall, he recognizes it's time to shine a light on his own strengths and weaknesses regarding spending & saving, planning & implementing, investing, and so on. Time to be Open Book about all of it in his marriage with Elisabeth. It's personal and gritty work that he's assuredly up to, though he wishes he'd embarked on it some years back. As for Elisabeth, her disappearance during that seven-year stint is a bit of mystery. Perhaps personal finances did not interest her. Perhaps she simply trusted Paul. I don't know her well enough to really comment.

What I do know is that scores of folks are ambivalent if not anxious about fully engaging their spouses on financial matters for fear of conflict. Not the most effective response to a challenging situation, but arguably quite rational AND accurate.

Obviously no one likes conflict. That's a given. But here's another given, or so I will assert: Money is inherently provocative. Not evil, not the devil; but, yes, highly provocative, highly inclined to induce opposition in marriage. The reason is that it brings out all manner of individual differences, arguably like nothing else in marriage. And this seemingly ordinary fact creates layers of complexity that consistently catch us unawares in the partnership, unless and until we get hip to what's going on. Then we can manage the differences. Then we can tame them. Managing our money well will still be a great challenge, but we won't be our own worst enemy. Let us therefore put this story of differences into greater relief.

MONEY IS THE DEFIANT EXCEPTION

Social psychologists tell us *like-kind* is the rule in love, in mate attraction and selection. I know, it all sounds a bit animalizing, but actually it seems plausible when you think about it. Seeking like-kind—consciously, unconsciously, or somewhere between—is something we humans do and it seems to be a near-universal organizing principle in social life and especially in selecting a life partner. In common parlance, we know this as "birds of a feather flock together." Affinities bind. With our family and circle of friends we usually share some healthy dose of the following: core values, notions of what is fun and funny, socioeconomic status and ambitions, locale, friends, political views, mannerisms, even looks. Social psychologists have dubbed this phenomenon "positive assortment."[9] It lubricates connection, and naturally lends itself to relationship harmony and stability. In life it's quite comforting to be amongst "our people."

Even so, money rebels. It goes against the flow of positive assortment. It is a phenomenon where differences are the norm.

Consequently for most of us an array of relationship work is to be done. It needn't be glum. It's not punishment for sinners. Do consider: Differences between partners—untended, unexamined—do tend to stoke conflict and misunderstandings. True, differences may be the spice of life, but these differences need to be processed. They need to be cooked. Beans are great, pork is tasty, and so on, but uncooked—not so much. They require the heat, the mindfulness, the exertion, and the skill of cooking before we can enjoy them. In relationship terms, this calls for cheerful exertion and skill.

The *Lion Hearted Love* approach unflinchingly asserts, *Differences are fine, differences are welcome, and money should be regarded as a welcome catalyst for the ensuing partnership work; namely, consciously integrating the wide array of psychic and practical elements that money activates and brings into play.* For now, though, let's come back to the phenomenon itself—that there are differences. To do so, we'll make use of a quirky yet fun study on how partners can be so different on one of the most ordinary levels of personal finance—spending and saving. Scores of other dichotomies and distinctions are to be found in the domain of money and marriage, but I think the following microeconomics piece should quite nicely illustrate the point.

PAIN AND PLEASURE

Folks have remarkably different attitudes to budgeting, to really looking at their spending habits, and—surprise, surprise—folks report having remarkably different *internal* experiences when out and about, spending their dollars. There's a peculiar 2008 study made by an interdisciplinary academic team of two economists and a psychologist from Northwestern University and University of Pennsylvania's Wharton School of Business, and published under the rather droll title, "Tightwads and Spend-thrifts."[10] The study examines the decision-making processes and spending experiences of consumers. Pain and pleasure, saving and spending: This is one very busy hub of human behavior, personal finance, and emotion. Some of us are inclined to habitually save our money; others are inclined to habitually spend it. A few of us consistently occupy the elusive middle. What underlies these basic behaviors? *Pain and pleasure,* assert the authors. I myself find it absolutely fascinating that individuals—friends, family, lovers, members of the same church, synagogue, or meditation center—can have more or less the same objective experience (i.e., buy a crisp Gala apple; pay for dinner at Slanted Door; move money from checking to savings account) and yet inwardly experience the transaction so differently from one another.

Peruse, for starters, the group that the "Tightwads and Spendthrifts" study identifies as savers. What motivates them to save? As the saver universe is bifurcated, the answer is twofold. Some folks delight in saving and thus are moved by the sheer delight of it. Another group, however, holds tight to its money in order to avoid the emotional pain of parting with it. For them, spending hurts. The purchase could be a diamond as big as The Ritz, or as mundane as lunch for four at Salvaggio's Delicatessen.

"Sandwich, soda, and chips for you and the family— that's fifty bucks," the heavy-set deli man grunts. Marvin reaches for his wallet, thinking how the family should have stayed home and done this for 12 bucks. What were they thinking? Marvin pays the unshaven, burly man behind the counter. He can't stand such scenes and would like to avoid them if at all possible. But it's not possible. His wife and kids LOVE Salvaggio's prime rib.

Are we having fun yet? Well, no. Within the group of savers who save to avoid pain, there is a further subset for whom the most intense negative emotions occur *in anticipation of* the actual moment of transacting. Think about that: A person is at the farmers' market, in the delicatessen, clothing store, mega-super store, car dealership, what have you; he is there to make a purchase, one which for the sake of argument he can afford (i.e., it will not put him in the poor house, nor will it put his financial house in disarray); nonetheless, his emotional stress is greatest at the thought of parting with his cash *before* he has done the actual spending deed. Let's not even try to think what his wildly protesting mind thinks during such times! Evidently, some folks really put themselves through it as a part of their spending ritual.

As for the academic study itself, I'm not a fan of the overarching *Tightwad* expression because it is too much of a pejorative, at times feels like a parody, and thus leaves little room for the real-life degrees of discernment and frugality that certain individuals possess. Still, it's interesting to look at personal money through the very human lens of pain and pleasure. Without getting caught up in the sanity v. neurosis discussion of this—i.e., is this pain intrinsically neurotic or intelligent?—I do believe a smart (homeopathic) dose of the Tightwad's discomfort functions like an alert gatekeeper, ensuring that conscious and not impulsive spending decisions are made.

At the other end of the spectrum is the Spendthrift, that profligate spender who, like Sir Winston Churchill, is obviously not experiencing pain and probably taking great pleasure at the very time of his/her shopping activities. For this crowd, it's as if money is less real, less substantial than for the saver crowd. The forms and rules of money lose badly when going up against these passionate people, with their zest for experiences, their desire to live in the right neighborhood with the best schools, and the joys that come with acquiring cool and beautiful things. Theirs might be expressions of vapid materialism, but more often are reflections of a real passion for living. Again, without getting caught up in the sanity v. neurosis view of this, I think a dose of this style is desirable—especially as an antidote to parsimony and hoarding. Because, as everybody knows, *You can't take it with you.*

The academic researchers also draw a couples-and-money conclusion from their study. Tightwads and Spendthrifts apparently end up marrying each other with notable frequency. The researchers dub this phenomenon "Fatal Attraction." This pessimistic view of what happens when opposites come together is based in social psychology's premise that people get along best and easiest with their like-kind (aka positive assortment). Differences between spouses, as discussed, pose challenges to the relationship. This dynamic obviously stands out conspicuously when people are opposite in the extreme. But what about those who bring to the partnership a lighter touch at being "tight" with money? What about those with a lighter touch as "spenders?" I'm not sure what the authors of the study would say, but in this softer version of things I become a big fan of *differences*. For, in these cases there is tremendous potential for such couples to artfully organize operations by employing the specific strengths of personnel (that'd be themselves). One person might periodically offer a pinch of wakefulness (pain!), offsetting her partner's modes of over-exuberance and impulsivity. The other spouse might have them quaff down the occasional dram of nectar (pleasure!), dispelling his partner's parsimony, reminding them to let go every now and again, to be sure to enjoy the festive side of life.

Right now, I'd like to veer back to perusing the extremes as they offer us Characters by which to think about all this and perhaps evaluate ourselves, albeit light-handedly and by moderating degrees. Of course, these extreme Characters don't comprise the majority of folks out there, but there are enough of them, and the thing is, it only takes one wild person in a partnership to make a whole lot of chaos. To that end, we'll pay a visit to England and Sir-You-Know-Who, followed by a vintage 1980's vignette of college life and one notorious cat by the name of Vance Malkovich.

Chapter 19 Spenders

Do spenders—real, live, robust spenders—know that they're spenders? I think only *kind of*. Do real live robust spenders get feedback that they're spenders? I imagine that many do receive such feedback, perhaps with some frequency. But does it stick? Doesn't seem to. Doesn't seem to change them. What about budgets? Do budgets help? Usually not, at least in my experience. Now I don't see some huge *conscious* rebellion on the part of these spender types. It's strange and subtle what they're up to: They don't seem to fight having and doing a budget, but they don't exactly help the process along either!

Consider a large subgroup of spenders. They're what I called—in the *Zen Money Blues* typology—Planner Types. That is, these folks are constantly hatching plans. They're good at it. They like it. It's their identifiable strength. And they're consistently flexing that muscle. They make plans for the day, the week, and next year's holidays; for clothes, for meals; to have fun with friends; AND those plans require financial resources. Planners also think about retirement, insurances, contingencies, as well as all the awesome, connecting, and enriching experiences that money can buy (home, education, travel). That said, some Planner Types display a great difficulty with planning for the long term, because they are so absorbed and impassioned with the present. As such, they know for instance that they should have and work a budget, and they know they should have savings goals and consistently fund those goals. But they don't. They fail to prioritize. Their implementation is weak.

How do spender-planners regard themselves, therefore? Perhaps it comes as no surprise that they really don't perceive themselves as spenders, because they're making plans! Think about it. Making plans is the primary activity, followed by making those plans happen. Whether they can afford them, whether the implementation is efficient, whether the time is ripe—those practical realities are low, too low, on the list. The phrase, *Money is no obstacle*, comes to mind. Well, with that m.o., money will plainly become Personal Obstacle #1. And that's where the spender-planners get into trouble. That's how they make repeat mistakes— that, and the reality that this type is incredibly willful. In regards to lifestyle, and by proxy, money, these good people have been known to get awfully stubborn, if not intractable. They want what they want. And this can blind. Sir Winston had no issue putting his wife and children on a severe budget, but heaven forbid he lowered the boom on the real culprit—himself! Ah, ego. Ego can have its pride. Ego can have its blind spots. Ego can have its willfulness. As for the antidote to this, there's nothing surefire or easy, but later I will go with the hair-of-the-dog-that-bit-me approach. First though, let's see what we might be up against.

SIR WINSTON AND THE FAMILY PURSE

Between a wild and fetishistic annual requirement for fresh silk undergarments (cost in today's dollars about $2,500/yr)[11] and the endless expenditures of running their country home in Kent, Sir Winston Churchill knew how to spend, and spend he did. His personal financial world might rightly be summed up this way: *He wanted what he wanted. Period. End of story.* Real life of course doesn't end with such definite, emotional punctuation. Neither does money itself seem to respond one iota to bullying or willfulness: When you're out of dough, you're out of dough.

Willfulness is not inherently bad, of course. On the contrary it is essential in matters of genius and great achievement. But in matters of personal money and relationship, we will do well—as they say in the London underground—to *Mind the gap.* To take heed. To not be too enamored of our self when it is on autopilot. A homeopathic dose of humility isn't a bad idea, moreover. Need I say the latter was certainly not Winston's strong suit?

The years-on blend of willfulness and myopic planning style finally caught up with him. Indeed, it rather rained on his parade. The year was 1947, not 24 months after the Allies had prevailed in the Second World War. The subjects of Her Majesty's kingdom, weary of war, wanted a fresh prime minister. Thus Churchill was voted out of 10 Downing Street. Worse, he was also plumb out of money. Broke. So broke he could not afford to keep Chartwell, the family home in the country, his refuge, his salve, his throne, and his delight for over two decades. What happened?

In the years and decades prior to his premiership, Churchill had been a prolific writer and journalist, enjoying a rabid following in America as well as the UK. This side career of his was the income generator that time and time again had saved his financial bacon. Problem was, circa 1939, the world needed saving. This required Churchill's every waking moment for the next six years. Writing was out of the question, obviously. At the same time the stipend for PM (prime minister) was modest, at least relative to Churchill's unedited spending habits. As a result, in 1947 he found himself without office, without publishing income, and deep in debt. It had all come home to roost. Chartwell had to go.

There is more to the story of Chartwell, going back to the beginning, regarding the circumstances by which it was acquired, including Winston's egregious marital faux pas, his indelicately overriding Clementine's misgivings about purchasing it. Suffice to say, his plan was rather inauspiciously executed. Meantime, Sir Winston strutted through life, ever the passionate planner of and for today! Long-term financial plans, or plans for contingencies, say, in the event that he were called upon to be a world hero and therefore could not make a buck writing articles? Such personal financial plans were nowhere to be seen. As history reads, Churchill was uncannily prescient in matters of global conflict, of the clashes between nations and the malevolent forces that would play out in the first half of the 20th century. In the more modest region of his home and family finances, however, Churchill displayed none of that acumen or foresight.

The story doesn't have a wretched ending, luckily. Several friends of the family did come to the fore in 1947 and purchased Chartwell for the benefit of the National Trust, with the covenant that Winston and Clemmie could live out their days there. This, Winston did, enthusiastically. Clemmie would leave shortly after Winston's death, however. For, much as she loved Chartwell, it also was for her a four decades' financial thorn in her side—even if it possessed the most lovely gardens imaginable.

My professional experience with the very willful spender-planner type is that he will wear you down, unless and until he sees the cliff. As an advisor I do have a few tricks up my sleeve. Much better, though, is when his beloved partner lowers the boom—

lovingly but intensely. In such instances, particularly when too much control of the purse has been ceded to the spender, I've seen partners do what can only be described as, *Get Churchillian! Fight the good fight!* Indeed, a whole chapter could be devoted to fighting smart and fighting fair regarding matters of marriage in general, and personal money in particular. But I'll spare you. Still, there is a time to fight the good fight in relationship—especially in regards to issues of money, control, and those who are out of control. But it has to be done right. Care and forethought are absolutely critical. Our words had best be spot on, or it could get bloody. Winston got to hide behind the patriarchy. No one gets to do that now. Not patriarchy, not matriarchy. As for the best place to fight the good fight, I think the Kula-type partnership meeting is the perfect venue. No need to ambush. Just prepare well, be armed with good information and a sharp analytical mind, and present the facts. Fight the good fight. That fight must be won. Don't hesitate. This may be your best chance to right the ship, to eschew mediocrity. Jolly good luck.

Chapter 20 Aristocratic Blues

We just opened the book on the willful spender-planner type who can look fun, normal, even be a great hero, yet leave financial havoc in his wake. The fundamental issue for the Sir Winstons of the world is their conspicuous refusal to prioritize. They're unwilling, if not insulted, that they're required to cut some agendas out, or to put other agendas on the back burner. It's a sort of adolescent protest, one that kings and queens and aristocratic families have performed time and time again, with recognizably disastrous consequences. This want-it-all willfulness is difficult, if not exhausting to defend against. The spender-planner just loves living the dream, is attached to each and every detail of it, and nothing is going to slow him down—not money, not those "stuffy" notions of prioritizing. In marriage, he is the classic overspender who periodically stresses everybody out, except perhaps himself. Over the long run this intransigence has been known to play rather badly in marriage.

Cinema and fiction tend to offer us the more charming and fun version of this Character. Therein, he feasts on all that life has to offer, rubs elbows with the rich and famous, or makes sure his family has every comfort and convenience. In all cases money is no obstacle. Until it is! Then the Great Depression arrives, or mishap befalls this Charming Character. Suddenly, he is confronted with the prospect of losing it all. It's scary, and time to hunker down and survive, as it were. But the real life story of this Character is rarely that condensed or obvious. Much more, it's about how many small overages make for one very depleted purse down the road of life. On occasion, its effects might not be felt for decades!

Consider the financial state of British aristocracy in the second half of the 19th century: Victoria's empire was in full bloom but many of the centuries-old lordly families were—after generations of mismanagement and, I imagine, some lavish lifestyles and sumptuous soirées—broke. Winston Churchill's family was among them. Shrewdly, a number of young aristocrats of that era, including Churchill's father, took American brides. These ladies later became known as Dollar Princesses. They belonged to the wealthiest families stateside, and to this day many historians believe that it was their families' infusion of cash that got the British aristocracy through a very rough patch. Which is not to say that Winston Churchill, or those who loved him (i.e., his American mother, Jennie, and later his wife, Clementine), would be spared the stressful consequences of his lifelong habit of overspending.

Does this diminish Churchill's greatness? As noted earlier, that's a relatively silly question. The man might not have been able to save two pence, thereby making those in his world emotionally bonkers, but he displayed leadership and oratorical powers that saved Western Civilization from the brink of profound darkness. And therein lies one of life's contradictions. The spender-planner (immature and willful in the extreme) can be found among the most positive, courageous, and charismatic people you'll ever know, while simultaneously indulging a dark move that not-so-charmingly threatens to spend the family out of house and home. *Sir Winston on a budget?* Good luck with that one. The guy was a tough nut. Still, I suspect things would have taken a very different trajectory (China plates included) had he and Clemmie lived in these modern, egalitarian times. I can't help but envision a modern Clementine Churchill calling him to account, and taking control of the family purse. Of course we'll never know for sure, now will we?

Chapter 21 Savers

Now we open the book on the other guy, the one for whom budget is not a dirty word, the one for whom the value of a nickel and a dime is quite tangible. It's reflected in the rigor with which he parts with his cash (i.e., spends), and it's reflected in his capacity to stash cash away (save). In a trice we'll survey the genuine brilliance of this saver-implementer Character, followed by an exploration of how, on occasion, he can be seriously skewed. But first an important cautionary note which I hope is altogether unnecessary: The idea that some folks are much better than others at certain facets of personal finance is NOT to be confused with the modern ethos that each partner has equal status in marriage. Each partner does. Nothing undercuts that. Or rather, nothing in *Lion Hearted Love* should undercut the shared journey aspect of love and marriage. Money is in service of love. Always. Partners had best talk. Even if one person is widely regarded as All-Universe at finding a deal on a brand new automobile—the latest VW, let's say—it is nevertheless prudent to be in sync with one's partner. When such a person is not, or he simply doesn't bother, it then turns a personal strength into a relationship weakness. God forbid his partner is not into VW's.

The upcoming Vance Malkovich vignette depicts the saver-implementer in action, going too far and taking more control than he ever should be allowed. Saver as troublemaker? Read on! In the extreme such a person has been known to become intoxicated with saving, obsessed with a deal, and—now we hit his penchant for overreaching—he has frequently believed that *getting deals is excellent planning itself!* As for the implementer side of the equation, Vance Malkovich belongs to that rather large subgroup of savers who possess the implementer's finest chops—they know how to smartly spend. It's a natural fit for many savers. After all, one key to saving is not simply to refrain from spending, but to spend well. When we spend effectively, and get something cool for a very good price, then we of course have money left over. *Voilà* savings! The logic of this is apparent. But the cognitive-emotional underpinnings aren't something we think a lot about. Some folks enjoy a good deal and feel lighthearted about ending up with a little change. But others, *Watch out!* They love, indeed, they *demand* a good deal and *demand* a little change as well. Consider this short from our recent summer holiday in Maine.

This morning, it rains. That means Plan B. My wife and I will make a small excursion, walking the 400 yards from our cabin to the holiday gift store. Our nine-year-old nephew wants to come. Before we head out, he gets 10 bucks from his dad so he can buy something. All the way to the store, through that haze of Maine rain, the wee lad has his hand in the pocket with the ten-dollar bill. He has an extra hop in his step. Once at the gift store, however, our otherwise well-mannered nephew makes repeated expressions of displeasure (you know, a sour face). This is strange. My wife seeks an explanation. There are murmurings, then an upshot. The wee lad wants to purchase something with the 10 bucks his dad gave him BUT he most definitely also wants some money left over. To that end, he wants to negotiate with the shop lady about the cost of the merchandise on the shelves! So as not to offend, my wife has a stealth conversation with the shop lady, who responds with a great laugh: "Bring the little negotiator on!" Indeed, our nephew ends up getting his gift and his change, too. But here is the mysterious part. As we have known our nephew's mom and dad for a long time, we can safely assert that this behavior was neither taught nor encouraged. Nor has it been particularly modeled by them. (Did I say that out loud?)

Uncontrived moments such as these certainly give rise to lively questions. From whence do such strong preferences come? How much is a reflection of nature, how much of nurture? Personal financial education and family inculcation are undeniable factors, but are they overrated? What about how we tick? What do we already bring to the personal money game in the way of deeply rooted psychological styles? History serves up Sir Winston as a willful spender. Change him? Unlikely. Contain him? Perhaps in this modern time. Now at the other end of the spectrum, we will encounter Vance Malkovich. History doesn't know him, but I sure do. This guy is powerfully frugal. Change him? Unlikely. Contain him? We'll see.

Chapter 22 Being Vance Malkovich

In the right spot at the right time, like when you are 19 and rambling through Europe on $5/day, your *saver-implementer* pal is a hoot, is a terrific ally, and might just be All-Universe in the resourcefulness department. In the quotidian world, give this chap a budget and specific instructions, and he'll work it hard. Equally shiny is his protector energy. He's a natural saver. He's a superb implementer. Further on down the road of life, he'll likely be the one in charge of the family purse.[12] Grabbing the controls comes naturally for him, in part because he's good at paying the bills, approving expenditure, and doling out allowances. He regularly tunes into what's in the bank and what bills are coming down the pike. All in all, he likes engaging on these levels. In consumer mode the guy knows price and quality, and is a font of great ideas. In a passionate moment we might call him brilliant and clever. However, this Character has been known to take his singular agenda (and control) too far. This could lead to strange outcomes. Some kinds of strange outcomes are stranger than others. No doubt, the following is a story that belongs at the far end of the saver-implementer universe.

As an aside, I am not sure exactly how prevalent the more extreme Characters are. Clearly they're out there. But I present them primarily for pedagogical and rhetorical purposes. Extreme examples are vivid. As unsubtle points of reference, they orient us, and—I hope—get us thinking about our own style, as well as our particular strengths and weaknesses. If we can muster a laugh or two, and do it in good fun, then all the better. The following is just such a mirthful account. When a saver-implementer-in-the-extreme is given free reign on both the planning and implementing side of life, things can get kooky fast. Introductions thus are in order. Meet my former travel buddy and college roommate, Vance Malkovich. His antics are as funny as they are forgivable. Chalk it up to youth. But the thought of Vance Malkovich doing some variation of his 24/7 overweening frugality *in marriage*—to that, I say we should take a moment, bow our heads, and pray for his bride: *May she be self-sufficiently wealthy, or may she be terribly clever. Or both! Amen.* Now then, please do sit back and enjoy the weirdness.

ONE LONG LINE OF WEIRD

We were 19 with no car payments,[13] getting our first and unforgettable taste of life as a Moveable Feast. Seemingly made for this was Chambéry, an idyllic small city in the French province of Savoy, surrounded on all sides by the Alps. Back in the day, a gaggle of us CU Boulder students did spring semester there. It was glorious. It was also here that I met Vance Malkovich for what would be a semester to pal around, ski as often as possible, imbibe 8-franc table wines to die for, consume large quantities of smelly cheeses, fruit, and baguettes—and take a few university classes to make the whole trip legit.

It was 1982, Ronald Reagan was president, the *International*

Herald Tribune was still worth reading, and the US dollar stunk to high heaven. Resourcefulness, like a Swiss army knife, was therefore a requirement, as we all had to make our respective allowances last. In this regard, Vance excelled.

On Easter holiday break, he and I hit the road, and I got a firsthand look at his financial *savoir-faire*. We hitchhiked across the country, from Chambéry to Bordeaux, catching rides from one pensioner-packed Deux Chevaux after another. The plan was no-plan. As the spirit moved us. Or, wherever our driver was headed! One day that landed us at a weird heavy metal music festival in Angers. Not top of my list of things to do, but hey. Camping was our mainstay, camping anywhere and everywhere along the way—roadsides, parks, vineyards. Traveling on next to nothing, we were, and it was the height of cool. Who said a Moveable Feast had to be extravagant? Just give us the French countryside!

And then my first taste of life as a Moveable Feast came to a close. It was time to deal with the real world again. Fall semester in Boulder was fast approaching, and we needed to find a place to live. This was worrisome. Finding good housing in Boulder was not easily done from afar. Best was to be there in person, to scour the listings, look at a lot of funky places in hopes of landing that one decent abode. But Vance was on it. He was the man. He needed a place, too, and so did a buddy of his. *Why don't we all three get a place?!* Awesomeness was on the rise. And getting better: Since Vance was both from Colorado AND the man, he offered to do yeoman's service that summer, tripping down to Boulder till he found us a pad. Amazingly, he got the deed done in one day. Talk about awesomeness.

I couldn't wait for the year to begin.

Well, I really could have.

You know how it is when you rewind something in your

mind and a line stands out that failed to in real time? Later, you rewind and replay and wince at how you missed it. Regretfully, that's how it was for me with Vance's, "Yep, the price is right." This was the word I got from him whenever he told me about our new digs. Not: "Great yard, nice porch. Pretty girls walk by there all the time." No, it was, "Yep, the price is right."

After two and a half days of driving west, I got to town on Labor Day, and found my way to our new digs on the east side of Boulder. *Hmmm, interesting.* Not exactly what I had in mind. For a brief moment I hoped I'd gotten the directions wrong. No such luck. As I pulled into the driveway of our new digs, I saw that the front yard was rife with round rocks, painted green. This was not good. Now schlepping my stuff round back (the entrance was in the rear), I was about to learn for the first and last time in my life what "garden level" apartment meant. This was not good, either.

Vance greeted me at the door, oddly gracious, like a southern aristocrat on the veranda welcoming a weekend guest. Only there was no veranda and no guest. Vance started to look different to me. It was hard to say how. Perhaps it was the light, or lack thereof, as he escorted me under a ceiling of pipes and past a couple of plywood doors. Part tour guide now, Vance pointed at the doors, and touted the internationalism of our neighbors: one of them was Polish and recognized as a great swiller of vodka, the other guy—well, I stopped listening. For, in that wan light of the basement of what had to be the ugliest pad in the prettiest college town in America, I caught a glimpse of the deeper recesses of the mind of Vance Malkovich, and it was truly bizarre.

Vance was proud. This was a sort of victory lap for him.

But the bizarreness almost made sense, almost bordered on cohesion, after I surveyed the layout of our new pad. *Oh, my!* There was one window for the whole apartment, a 2' x 3' piece of dirty plexiglass facing north, letting scant light into the bedroom that Vance and Luke would share. My windowless bedroom was a piece of work. Mostly finished, it was, except down at the base of the drywall, where the foundation was exposed. The main room was, shall we say, multipurpose, with a couch for chilling. The Crockpot lived here, too, on top of the mini-fridge. What need for a kitchen when you have a Crockpot? The room reeked of lentils. I would get used to it. A lot of lentils would be cooked during the six weeks that we inhabited this godforsaken hovel.

Indeed, it was a time to be philosophical, to gain perspective, to learn non-attachment, to be a student of life! This, I did. In addition to learning that lentils are not among my favorite dishes, I also learned that you have to carefully remove every single tiny pebble that's hiding among them in raw form, or find yourself, like Luke did, at the dentist's with a cracked tooth. Driving Luke to the dentist one afternoon in need of urgent attention—that, to me, was further elaboration on what a bizarre financial universe the Zealously Frugal can create and perpetuate. I suppose you could say he should have been more aware, though I can't recall—before or since—eating a meal that *might* have rocks in it. Can you imagine going to dinner at your favorite neighborhood restaurant and inquiring of the waitperson: *Does the King Salmon have rocks in it tonight?* In the end Luke had to fork out hundreds of bucks to get his tooth crowned after noshing on the aforementioned ill-fated twenty-cent serving of lentil & pebble stew.

Regarding Vance Malkovich, it was one long line of weird. At this point I have to confess that Being Vance Malkovich, being a denizen in his realm, was quite voluntary. I did not have to stay there. My mom, apprised of the situation, was all for me bailing and finding fresh, respectable living quarters on the right side of town. But you can't fix stupid, as they say. While I was 19 and without a car payment, I was also 19 and the neural wiring in my frontal lobe was not complete, either. Oddly intrigued with Being Vance Malkovich, I thus hung around.

Turns out our days in the hovel with the green painted rocks in the front yard were numbered. But first I needed an extra serving of humble pie, and while we're at it, why not also involve my girlfriend? Kisty was cool, fortunately. To bring a girlfriend back to the hovel with the green rocks on 30th Street was, I suppose, a sort of test. Kisty passed muster. Or, more correctly, I passed muster with Kisty, who liked me in spite of my digs. How lucky was I? What a girl. She liked me for who I was, not what I had. That is, until one morning my head itched.

Heading over (no pun intended) to the student health center that Saturday morning, I knew where this was going. A month of sleeping on a futon next to the hovel's exposed foundation could not be the paragon of hygiene in Western civilization, or Boulder. In the course of my getting examined by the doctor, she wanted to know if there were others with whom I had had intimate contact. Ouch! Well, suffice it to say I left the health center that morning with fine-tooth combs and special shampoo for two. Kisty was a brick. A lovely earth goddess of a girl from Lawrence, Kansas, she just laughed the whole thing off.

Our time in the hovel on 30th Street came to a swift, climactic close one Saturday night just before Halloween when the pipes in the ceiling above burst. There was a great spray of water and an inch of it on the floor and Vance salvaged the Crockpot and I threw my clothes in a backpack and loaded up my toys in the car and never looked back. Of course, we now needed a new place to live, and this time Luke, not Vance, was in charge of the expeditionary forces, landing us a better pad for a reasonable sum in the right part of town where they still used green grass as the element of choice for a front yard. My yen for being Vance Malkovich filled, I moved on.

. . . .

Returning to the present, let's imagine Vance doing his thing in the context of the marital partnership. This time, instead of searching for an abode for himself and his college buddies, he takes on the emotionally amped up project of buying (or building) a new home. In the cool-meets-mature scenario, where Vance manifests as non-extreme implementer and deal seeker, harmonizing with the lead of his talented and smart planner-type spouse, he will doubtless be The Man. She'll provide him with neighborhood parameters and house specs: *No, to University Hill—it doesn't feel safe for our little girls. No, to Gunbarrel, it's too far from town and friends. Yes, to Newlands because of safety and schools and proximity to town, and, yes, it's fine if we then have a smaller house because the prices are higher there!* The saver-implementer type with a focused plan like this is just so dang potent. Vance will do the due diligence with the house inspector; he'll relish the full-contact negotiation with the sellers; he'll ask his future neighbors about traffic and the schools—and this rigor will pay dividends.

But conjure for a moment a less harmonious world where our Vance-like character defies—perhaps quietly defies—the parameters of spouse or planner-type advisor. He does love his wife, but after she meticulously puts forward her ideas on what best suits them and why, he works against her. Firstly, as she is not like him—i.e., she's a spender—he feels he has a duty to protect their savings from her less than efficient visualization of their next home. There is both some truth and some arrogance in his view of her. All the while, he believes he knows what's best. Should he go Open Book? *Why? I'm right!* Proof is in his mind and on the net worth statement. *A home is an investment. End of story.* Working at cross-purposes, he'll pursue his agenda, seeking the "best deal," based on his personal formula of what "best deal" is, all the while slyly discounting the wants and needs of others. Relationship-wise, this is not good. Practically speaking, the new house could prove odd for the inhabitants, and become a constant source of irritation. If our Vance-like character is not careful, he could find that net worth statement (the one of which he is so proud) cut in half, minus divorce attorney fees and perhaps taxes. It happens all the time. Then he will have violated what I consider the First Rule of financial planning for married couples: Take care of your marriage.

Not surprisingly, the saver-implementer is the least likely person to be a financial house afire. But unaware of his shadow side, he may build a house of resentment. All of the people in his world, except him, can see his affliction of price myopia. Or, as the Oscar Wilde quote goes, "He knows the price of everything and the value of nothing."[14] The pent-up demand in his spouse or children or parents, the pent-up demand for living and individual expression is something he just doesn't see, not where money is concerned. He just doesn't register—or severely discounts—that others have hopes and dreams that are dear to their hearts; hopes and dreams quite apart from saving and deal making. This makes for a strange prison of schisms. Heaven help the day when the prisoners revolt.

Chapter 23 Open Book (Redux)

When we relax *ego* enough to vet—without fanfare or protest—the individual strengths and weaknesses of our self and our partner, we turn a critical corner and leave behind behaviors that portend mediocrity and repeated setbacks. Victory is not assured, of course. But this sort of Odyssean practicality, this sort of *emotional intelligence*, this willingness to see past the potential distortions of who we think we are, of who we want to be, and fearlessly go Open Book—this brings with it tremendous protection: psychological protection (we are more trustworthy in our decision making), relationship protection (our spouse from time to time is able to bury the hatchet), and economic protection (the team will make fewer errors, will solve more problems, and that can't be wrong). The goal is to day-in and day-out field the best team, put each one of us in the position(s) that best suit us, and get support from others (friends, family, professional) to fill in any gaps, whether in the areas of planning, implementing, investing, or strategic life decisions. The means to this end: We make ourselves Open Book, first to our own self, then to our partner. Of course, as this HR approach pertains to our personal finances, we do this in the privacy of our home, and perhaps our financial advisor's office.

No doubt, relaxing ego is easier for some than for others. At least in this American culture, money remains especially charged for the modern male ego. It frequently serves as a measuring stick for manhood and male prowess and success, and that's complicated. Moreover, in regards to money and the modern male ego—it's not just about the guy having a lot of money in relation to his peers (and thereby gaining their respect and/or admiration). It's also strongly linked to handling it, talking about it, dispensing it, and perhaps even doing all of this with a flourish. Pick your metaphor: money can be a part of his rooster dance, it can be the shine on his warrior armor, and it can definitely be prop and proxy for his assertion of princely social standing. The stakes are high. Should a woman crimp his style, there might be real resentment, even implied accusations of emasculation. *Wait, you're putting me on an allowance? I can't buy the car I want when I want it? I can't tell our broker to put it all on red, I mean, black? I know how to invest. What's your problem?*

How this relates to women and the female ego is not clear to me. Are there women for whom social standing and self-worth are inextricably connected to money? Of course. But at present the studies show men badly acting out when financial and career matters go south: Incidence of domestic violence increases four fold with unemployment, and suicide (and depression) sadly wax during times of unemployment and financial duress.[15] I'm sure women feel the full effects of such hard times, but it clearly plays out differently for them. It does seem like women are much more psychologically flexible than men in these matters, but now I'm officially out of my league.

Relaxing ego, and vetting who's good at what, can also be

disconcerting for The Educated. *I went to good schools. Got my degree. Make good money. I'm not some lowdown loser who can't balance a checkbook. I mean, I can balance a checkbook, even though I never do. I keep meaning to hire someone to do that for me, but I'm really busy with my Fantasy Baseball League. Besides, hiring that person is like a full-time job itself. Good help is hard to find, you know.* But seriously, let's dig and delve here. The amount of education a person has achieved correlates positively to earned income. The more education you have, the more money you make. Studies repeatedly corroborate the veracity of this link of education to earnings power. In matters of personal finance as measured by the bottom line of net worth, however, there's no such confirmed link. Education evidently doesn't translate to greater net worth.[16] IQ doesn't either. Odd, isn't it?

Relaxing ego in regards to who we are in our personal money world can definitely be difficult for those folks who are quite successful in business, moreover. Being good at making money should mean we'll be good at managing it, right? But in real life and in the popular media we regularly encounter the opposite: People who make scads of money tear through it with none of the discipline that went into making it. In 2010 a *Wall Street Journal* writer, Robert Frank, wrote a book on billionaires called, *The High Beta Rich*. In it he asserts that the number of billionaires in America hasn't changed much in the past decade, but the turnover in this stratospheric segment was shockingly high. According to Mr. Frank, about 80% of billionaires fell out of billionaireness during the past decade.[17] Talk about First World problems! On a less rarefied note, we all know stories of entrepreneurs and professionals of law and medicine overextending themselves with the twin-turbo prop plane purchase, the killer cars, half-baked get-rich-quick investment schemes; or, to be fair, overinvesting in truly great ideas that get crushed by the large and impersonal forces of the global economy. Usually such misplays contribute to the long fall to financial mediocrity, rather than some cataclysmic personal financial event. As such, these miscues can easily be covered over and forgotten, until down the road when these folks wonder why they have less than they should given all their hard work.

To relax ego and see without psychological agenda—that is, I believe, the quintessence of emotional intelligence in this domain. It makes for psychological flexibility. If you need help in implementing a particular part of your financial plan (for instance, buying long-term care insurance), then you find someone who has that knowledge set. If you need help crafting an investment strategy that isn't too risky but puts you in a position to reach your goals, then you seek an investment savvy thought partner. If you and your spouse have topics (like the rest of us) that are incendiary, you don't have to keep leaping into that fire alone: Find someone to be the skilled facilitator, so you talk it through and reach an understanding in a civilized manner, ideally without injuring each other. Over the years I've heard several very accomplished psychotherapists say that 50% of treatment is *done* the moment the person reaches out and asks for help. I think a similar statement can be made regarding personal finances. Obviously this is a plug for the good guys—the seasoned financial professionals who love working closely with folks—but for me the statement goes far beyond that: I am a huge believer in the power of relationship (as opposed to the do-it-yourself model), especially in regards to managing personal finances, because I believe that it is *through* relationship that most of us learn and grow, educate ourselves and stay current, as well as follow through on what we say we're going to do.

Speaking of relationships, let us close with an anecdote concerning Sir Winston and his investment advisor, Bernard Baruch. It was 1930 and Churchill had been racing all across America giving speeches and generally promoting his books to an adoring public. Of course, the stock market had been in the throes of insane volatility since the Black Monday sell-off in October 1929. In the nine or so months after the Crash, Churchill "took control" of the situation, episodically and frantically calling in orders to Baruch's brokers, instructing them to sell various stock holdings and buy others. In regards to Sir Winston's investing behavior, the man was wild and intractable. Then came the moment of reckoning. It was time to return to England, and, by his mental accounting, he was flat broke. Baruch's people confirmed that, in light of Churchill's latest spate of trading, he had indeed lost it all. Churchill was beside himself. But, as they say, sometimes in life it's better to be lucky than good. Sir Winston should have been penniless, except that he had hired Bernard Baruch to manage his money—thus, Bernard Baruch had come to know how reckless and horrid Churchill's investor instincts truly were. Baruch had deftly devised a plan. He had his team take the other side of most every bet that Churchill made in that crazy period; so his team bought the stock holding when Churchill sold it, and vice versa. At the end of Churchill's losing streak, when Sir Winston was sure that he'd lost everything, Baruch gave him back his principal plus a little advice: Baruch told Sir Winston to hide his money under the mattress, dig a hole in the garden, what have you—just don't ever again invest it *by himself* on Wall Street!

ESSAY IV

BRASS
TACKS

Chapter 24 Even Thoreau Had One

Thus far we have dug into our own psychology, delved into the ways and means of our partner, and done this assiduously and deliberately, because money-in-marriage is not a go-with-the-flow proposition. It requires conscious effort. Here and there I've also penned a few notes on the brass tacks of personal money, mostly stuff around the edges on how money works, what it requires of us, regardless of our agenda, regardless of our virtue, regardless of our hopes and fears. Now we hit the topic of brass tacks squarely on the head. First, we'll perk up in matters of the budget. It's a bit more 3-D than we might think. Then there is the matter of prosperity. Time to rise to the occasion, to do some serious planning, or risk leaking our good fortune. Finally, there is the Dual Nature of Money. It is an ordinary insight to some, yet the grossest insult to others. It states: Managing personal finances is an endeavor quite apart from making money in the world. The implications of this are curious. Doubtless there are other brass tacks aspects to make note of, but let's let these suffice for now.

The point of this brass tacks discourse is this: *Use them. Apply them in all quarters of our personal financial world (i.e., spending*

& saving, planning & implementing, investing, and decision making). When we don't, we create friction and duress that are wholly unnecessary. That is thematic throughout this collection of observations and commentary. But let me be clear. Respecting money is not just for the rich and the ambitious. Indeed, it has nothing to do with the size of your bank account or investment portfolio. Just consider our old and dear transcendentalist friend, Mr. Henry David Thoreau. How does he begin his essays on life and nature and being and doing in his brooding meditation, *Walden*? Answer: With a rather fussy and boring and LONG list of financial accounts, in the appropriately titled Chapter 1: "Economies." If there ever were a person less moved by material possessions and societal status, it'd be Thoreau. Yet he also knew that the freedom of his life—his life of the mind, his life of the senses, his having the time to study and adore Nature—was predicated on being able to afford his life. Thoreau *respected* this brass tacks level. He treated money as neither more nor less than it was; namely, that money was a necessary element of his life that periodically deserved proper attention. Indeed, Chapter 1 of *Walden* is testament to this.

The subject of budgeting is where we'll recon first. It's the least cool element, the nebbish of personal finance, and definitely the least cool topic in this book. In the modern era, moreover, no civilian has ever excused him or herself from the raging fun Saturday night party, to go home and work on the budget. *Hey, guys. I'm outta here. I've got a date with a sweet gal named Excel. Can't be late. See ya!* The topic is universally unloved. Even from folks who write about personal finance for a living, the very folks from whom you'd least expect it: Budgeting has been known to get no respect. Too often it gets presented in facile terms that serve no one. I believe the expression is to dumb something down.

Regarding what budget and budgeting are, let's definitely not do that.

SIMPLE DOES NOT EASY MAKE

A while back, the *New York Times* personal finance writer, Ron Lieber, addressed the topic of how the current economic downturn is impacting families and their young adults in his piece, "When the Fledglings Return to the Nest."[18] At one point, the following interchange between father and adult son is captured in the article:

> "I don't know how to make a budget," said Jeb Hastings, who left college 18 months ago but is going back soon. "I'd imagine it's simple. There's this much in gas, and whatever." His father, John, chimed in immediately: "That is all there is to it. It's a piece of a paper from a legal pad."

Well, no, not really. Budgeting is not a one-night stand; it's a process. Assuming we have crafted a budget that is credible, there is then the very real matter of tracking what we spend. Whether by pencil on yellow pad paper, using Quicken on the laptop, or *mint.com* on the smartphone, we only make budgeting meaningful when we periodically look at comparison numbers—namely, budget versus actual expenses. What good is the best budget in the world if we don't know where we stand in relation to it?

By the by, the point of a budget is not to beat it. Ideally there is a savings goal amidst budget lines that correspond to living our life today. A smart and accurate budget is zen-like in its ordinariness: It encourages us to spend when it is time to spend, and to save when it is time to save. Recognizing which time is which is really no great shakes. To call that "artfulness" would be a gross overstatement, although it can make for peace and harmony. Mostly, this experience of being synchronized with our financial world is the result of manual labor—of really and truly doing a budget. You're up to date on your budget-to-actual numbers so you know that you do (or don't) have the funds set aside for purchasing that shiny pair of sandals. Maybe you're wealthy enough that a hundred dollar pair of sandals won't make or break your situation, but I think you get the point: We all have a price-point threshold where it is wise for us to stop and first know where we stand in relation to our budget before we make a serious purchasing decision.

One of the salient issues with budgets is that they're patently unrealistic. Sometimes this is so because folks feel a little sheepish at how much they spend and/or how much they really want to spend. Other times I think this is a reflection of maturity. By laying out all that one is currently spending money on—well, it's pretty denuding, and it frequently leads to personal moments of truth. Not being able to have it all, one is thus required to prioritize, keeping some elements on the front burner and putting the rest on the back burner. Or, in less mature fashion, one can revert to plausible deniability mode. I take no delight in dinging Sir Winston, but we're onto his act.

One common miscalculation in the initial crafting of a budget pertains to "extraordinary" items (as opposed to committed or ordinary expenses). Financial planners have countless anecdotes about folks who live their lives, year after year, innocently brimming over with "extraordinary" (aka unplanned) expenses. For many of these folks, it never fully registers that their life and its expenses are consistently greater than they acknowledge. Flying the kids and grandkids home at holiday time ain't cheap. Young adults might take longer to leave the nest than originally anticipated, and as we know, these cherubim are rarely low maintenance or low cost. Aging parents, at the other end of the life cycle, might be financially relying on their 50-something children for all sorts of thises and thats. More, I've seen folks who consistently made outsized philanthropic gifts, or helped out their siblings, yet held firm to the idea that they were just one-time gifts. Not! In all cases the prescription is to integrate extraordinary expense lines into the budget. But if done thoroughly, the question naturally arises: Will folks take the medicine that will surely follow such a dose of reality?

Budgeting in concept is simple. Folks are wont to speak of it in facile terms, as if solely comprised of basic math and common sense. Traditional Economics with its vaunted notion of Utility reinforces this view. However, once we humanize this equation—adding our intuitions, emotions, and non-rational modes—we end up with the much rounder definition of economics that my college professor once espoused: "Economics is the study of human beings who have *unlimited wants yet finite resources.*" Indeed, the human experience of allocating finite resources to satisfy a profusion of powerful wants and needs is anything but easy. That is why I have broached this ostensibly obvious topic: To counteract the tendency to distort what is a rather craggy lay of the land. Budgeting is not calculus, clearly. But it does require dexterous planning, emotional intelligence, and a heavy dose of manual labor—in addition to the aforementioned yellow pad and pencil.

Chapter 25 Whatever For?

Just last week I was in San Francisco meeting with a very clever chap, Leon, 63 years of age, healthy, loving his job as Chief Information Officer for a well established global high tech company, and generally loving life. He and his wife make close to 700K per year, and that earnings power looks repeatable, at least for a while. Significant funds have already been set aside for retirement, though the goal appears a bit underfunded. To be fair, they've got the option to cut back on lifestyle and retire sooner. How happy they would be with such a fallback plan is unclear.

In the course of our meeting I broached the topic of budget, wondering if Leon and his wife had one (and for that matter if they had a bookkeeper). Leon shot me a look and said in earnest: *Whatever for?* I said a few words on the matter, to which he replied: *I generally know where we stand. When it's time to tighten up, we do. Otherwise, we thoroughly enjoy what we've got going.* I pursued the topic a bit further but it was obvious Leon wasn't keen on the idea that he and his wife might benefit from having and working a budget. I let the matter drop, but continued the dialogue in my mind afterward: *Hey, Leon, keep living exactly the way you're living, but doesn't it make sense to SEE what you're spending JUST TO BE SURE that all is as it should be? Why trust "generally knowing where you stand?" Smart folks have made miscalculations before. The next five years are important. You're an information officer. You know the power of information.*

Leon wasn't interested. Perhaps he was the kind of person who habitually resisted change. Probably he instinctively avoided ceding any measure of control. Doing a budget and maintaining a bookkeeper and holding the periodic discussion with one's partner (and perhaps advisor/planner) would represent a huge change to the solo, mental pencil-on-the-napkin approach. Accountability and transparency, too, would change like night and day. Now in regards to Leon: Was his aversion due to willfulness? Yes, I think so. Was it due to his incredibly fast paced life? Probably. Overconfidence in his ability to see into the future? I do worry a bit on this, too. But hey, maybe he does have it all under control. Maybe I'll be right and he'll still be lucky. That'd be fine by me. At any rate, only time will tell.

Not everyone is like Leon, of course. Many folks are more than willing to change it up, to build a new routine that works for them, although what they are *changing to* should be realistic. The new groove should be energizing and most definitely ride the strengths of each person in the marriage. Sir Winston had a grand and impassioned vision for family life in the shire of Kent, England. His capacity to bring that vision about in a stable manner, however—to do it in a way that balanced agendas of the present with the future—was woefully lacking. Pardon the arrogance of 20/20 hindsight, but I think he would have benefited greatly from having in his employ a firm and disciplined controller of the purse: Someone to slow him down, to ensure that projects were prioritized, to get him to make the hard decisions based on where they financially stood, to make him make more realistic assumptions about his future earnings power, and to make him plan a little for the intermediate and longer terms. One imagines Winston would have hated that loss of complete control. Then again, in the political realm the man knew when to compromise and when to be unswerving, and he very much knew what it meant to take the long-term and at times unpopular political stance. Indeed, Winston needed just that sort of chap in his personal financial circle: A chap whom he would have, by turns, loved and loathed, not unlike England's rather lengthy and mercurial relationship to him. In a different era this imagined Keeper of the Family Purse might have been Clemmie, or might have been a friend or professional counselor for hire. Even so, in this new and improved iteration of doing the purse, Winston no doubt would have given this chap a real run for the money!

Chapter 26 Prosperity's Pop Quiz

Whether caring for our children or aging parents, or launching a career or bringing it to the next level, or taking the artist's path or the seeker's, or serving others in the community, life can be all consuming; and as such, many of us have—at one time or another—lived under the financial regime that might best be called the Implied Budget. When we're low on dough, we're low on dough; no big surprise, and we heed that basic fact—although some individuals have certainly pretended otherwise and run up nasty credit card balances. In the mode of the Implied Budget, our money is simply earmarked to support our life. Because there isn't a whole lot of *extra*, there aren't a whole lot of discretionary choices. And while our life might be headed in a chosen direction, in line with what's important to us, I dissuade you from thinking that is the same as having a financial plan. It's not. Still, there's no gainsaying: The mode of the Implied Budget (and no crafted financial plan) might suffice for a good long while.

In the case of Brit and Jen, it functioned without major incident for 22 years. Then Brit started killing it at work. In an

18-month period his salary and bonus doubled. Talk about a fillip to one's financial life. But will Brit and Jen recognize the import of the time? It should be no big deal, right? Nothing to it—except that I'd be a very rich man had I received a nickel for every time I've heard folks say, "You remember, Honey, how back in the day we used to make $35,000 a year and we did all right? Even saved a little. But now that we're making good money (i.e., four, five, or six times that), we can't keep up!" Sir Winston and Paul Marylebone missed the moment, to be sure. The latter two gentlemen certainly enjoyed the sweetness of career success, the distinction of being great earners, but they quietly assumed that because they were great earners, that'd make up for everything—like overspending and financial mismanagement. As we know for Sir Winston, not so. Regarding Paul, we shall see. And as for Brit and Jen, they're on it, thank goodness. It took but one wake up call, one flash of lightning and one crash of thunder, and then they recognized how the old regime of Implied Budget (*sans* plan) was not remotely going to fly in their new financial world order.

LIGHTNING FAST

All their married life Brit and Jen agreed on what's important: The marriage, the children, the arts, and quality of life. But that doesn't mean they'd automatically agree on what to do once Brit started taking home appreciably more money. As soon as there's *possibility* in the form of newfound, inherited, or earned extra money, it's amazing what that sets in motion. Suddenly, where there were no thoughts, there are now tons of thoughts! *What could we do with that extra bit of money? What could I, myself, do with that little windfall?* Not only that, one's partner can immediately appear as an obstacle to "my plan." The adversarial positioning to one another happens lightning fast. Scary fast. Even if the agenda isn't selfish, the point is that fresh modes of thinking and acting are called for.

This lightning fast dynamic caught Brit and Jen unawares. Up till now their financial world has been rather straightforward. For 22 years it was primarily guided by shared values, a shared vision for life. Family was the priority, followed by a real passion for the arts. By their own account, this set of values muted their earnings and career power. They were okay with that. As for what vaguely resembled a budget, their numbers went like this. After contributing to the 401k plan, covering the children's college tuitions, paying the mortgage, having a small backstop of saving, and living a "basic" life in Boulder, Colorado, there wasn't a whole lot of extra. The implied financial plan of this period was tangible and respectable: *Afford our life!*

Had life simply hummed along status quo plus for Brit and Jen, I believe we'd find them today still reasonably content. But no—the challenge came with prosperity. Brit had been hunkering down in his own career after the children left home. His star rose fast, though perhaps it was a long time coming. In less than two years' time his compensation doubled. Indeed, he was having fun and the money was ridiculously good. However, a nanosecond after Brit's income boost hit the joint checking account, Jen went on a *unilateral* spender bender. To be fair, it was a bender relative to the simple and frugal ways they'd heretofore lived by. Either way it caught Brit off guard. Jen had been talking in general terms about a long awaited trip, and then suddenly she had a plane ticket for herself, hotel reservations, and a robust itinerary for 9 days in Berlin, her favorite city for art, music, and no-nonsense bohemia.

Brit, knowing he was supposed to feel happy for her, felt quite mixed about it all. What irked him wasn't that Jen had plans, but that they were made without any formal discussion. He wasn't expecting her to ask him for permission, but he felt some kind of direct conversation between them was appropriate. The more he thought about it, the more it rankled him. Then he confronted Jen. I don't think Brit was at his diplomatic best. Conflict ensued. Brit suspects he was "kind of yelling" when he more or less conveyed the following: *We need a plan. When you return from Berlin, we need to make a budget and we need to make a plan. I don't want to be like those couples who never talk, who do whatever they please, and live far beyond their means because of it. That would depress me no end.*

Their clash lasted the better part of an hour, possessing more than a few fierce moments, but Brit and Jen would get to the other side of it. Working for them was a longstanding habit of fighting fairly, of not only respectfully attacking the other but being willing to cop to one's stuff at some point, too. In the end Jen had no problem with his request for better communication. She knew she'd jumped the gun out of sheer excitement and of course wanted his buy-in. Brit apologized for his first-rate fulmination. In the kitchen, the scene of the post-fight make up, there was the return of laughter and affection. As importantly, they had caught lightning in a bottle. That is, they were now wise to how fast *extra cash* set in motion all manner of new and exciting and electric ideas. In response to this they vowed to come together, to really bring mindfulness to what had become a very dynamic situation. No more implied budget, no more implied financial plan. Sir Winston and Paul Marylebone stumbled and fell right here. So be it. But not Brit and Jen. They caught on quick. They were synchronized now. That boded well for the next leg of their journey.

Chapter 27 The Guest that Never Leaves

Expectations in regards to accumulating greater and greater wealth can be sly. Even though we intellectually know the limitations of money, it's very hard to cut through the emotional expectations that wealth should deliver us *better* happiness and freedom from worry. Madison Avenue effectively and repeatedly hammers home this emotionally appealing message, so dubbed "financial freedom." I'm not a fan of the term, though I am an admirer of such handiwork. It's seemingly plastered everywhere. Flip through the *New Yorker*, the *Atlantic*, the *Economist*, or just about any quality publication and there it is: "Work with our asset management firm and we see a beach house in your future. This happy, chatty graying couple, sitting on the beach, *their beach*, rubbing footsies—that could be you. We got them there. Let us manage your wealth and we'll get you there, too." Only the message is skewed. While the financial firm itself may be reputable, wealth nonetheless remains no paradisiacal destination. For one, wherever we go, there we are! Wealth doesn't—presto!—liberate us from our own personal psychology. Miserable people know how to be miserable in the best of times. Rudderless marriages that were on the rocks probably won't suddenly find a rudder because there is now more wealth. It's possible, but I wouldn't count on that as a relationship tool chest. For two, freedom from worry is an absurd notion so long as we live and breathe in this human realm.

Of course having extra financial resources is a great boon to living our life fully. *That* goes without saying. But we can't expect the anxieties associated with personal finances to ever be solved once and for all. Wealth—whether we are accumulating it or we already have it—requires from us keener awareness. Better communication. Deeper reflection. Better checks and balances. Brit and Jen have some work to do. Best of all, they know it. They figured that out. Time to update their life goals and objectives, revise their financial plan, and at long last craft a formal budget —in that order. The days of seat-of-the-pants personal finance are over. Time to work anew the partnership. Their next life chapter has everything to do with harnessing their good fortune. It is imperative that they make the most of this propitious time.

Worry and anxiety are emotions we manage throughout our wealth experience. This is our job! This is psychological work! While meeting with success in the accumulation phase or having now created/inherited a pretty sweet nest egg, we should not be surprised or resentful that worries still visit us. True enough, material abundance will typically dispel those intense limbic layers of worry connected to *survival* in whatever socioeconomic world we live in. But those layers will be replaced by yet other layers of worry, responsibility, and insecurity. I don't think this makes money a co-conspirator in some cosmic joke played on us. Rather I think it's just part and parcel of what goes on in this personal money realm. As I've heard a Tibetan Buddhist lama put it: *If you own a horse, your worries are as big as a horse. If you own an elephant, your worries are as big as an elephant.* While certainly not a quantum statement about living amidst good fortune, I think this is one irrefutable aspect of it. Call it *prosperity worry.* It's the guest that never leaves!

Nor should we want said guest to leave. I regard a homeopathic dose of prosperity worry as normal, healthy, and medicinal. I don't mean to sound too clever. But consider Sir Winston. He could have benefited from a daily dose of prosperity worry, and I know that Paul Marylebone could have benefited from it. Both of them worried not one jot; that is, until moments of financial reckoning unceremoniously arrived. So, totally blocking or suppressing such worry is definitely not prescribed. Of course, there are the individuals who inhabit the other extreme. We all know them, people who worry obsessively about what they have. They regard their wealth as not enough. They want to make money investing but they don't want to lose money either. If the stock markets go up, it kills them that they're not in it full force. If the stock markets go down, they're freaking about what they do have in it. Some of these vicissitudes we all experience. But taken to the extreme, it is sadly neurotic. Somehow, we'd like to gain the middle. Find some solid ground. Equanimity. But even here, money is still wont to hit a nerve: *What if we blow our good situation? What if mishap befalls us? What if we conscientiously save, then die before we get to enjoy it?*

A homeopathic dose of prosperity worry, taken in the right place and at the right time, like when we're making investment decisions, could work rather nicely for us. A 2001 MIT study on investor behavior[19] corroborates this point. Data from thousands of trades at a retail brokerage firm were examined. Certain patterns emerged, perhaps most conspicuously among them: Women, whether in the group of married or single women, made the most profitable trading decisions as compared to the sub-groups of attached and not-attached men, and this was attributable, in part, to the fact that these women were generally not overconfident about their investment abilities. In action, that 'lack of overconfidence' translated into the women being more deliberate in their decision-making process, and that deliberation paid off in terms of fewer trades and better performance during the investment period.

The impact of gender on self-concept, in the study and in the world, is hard to miss. But whether in men or women, the identifiable enemy of effective long-term investing is psychological inflation. Fortunately, the antidote is in most cases quite basic. Some system of checks and balances is required. But this isn't always ready to hand. Consider the sub-group in the MIT Study who performed the worst: *Men, specifically those not in a serious relationship.* Now I'm not saying people should get into a relationship to become better investors, but there's no denying a good relationship with real accountability will—for many folks—counterbalance a tendency toward investor overconfidence. Relationship is seemingly made for these moments. It is extremely difficult to maintain a faulty self-concept (in this case, *of what a very fine investor I am*) when one's partner has the latest monthly brokerage statement in hand and wants to know why the value of the portfolio has gone down when the market went up. Variation on this theme: Some of us might never worry about money, per se, but we will worry about being confronted by our partner! That's all right, too.

Chapter 28 Midas Contemplates

From time to time, the weight and claustrophobia of our real-life commitments can make us unwilling to ask ourselves an existentially fundamental question or two: *Are we in the midst of a life well-lived? Have we taken a wrong turn?* This is not the purpose of this book, but the inquiry no doubt deserves its time and place. I mention it here because more than a few of us have embarked on a life journey with the Promised Land of financial freedom very much in our sights. At the outset such a pursuit was genuine if not a tad innocent. But then we get down the road of life and wonder if we'll ever get there. Perhaps we dread what we need to do to keep it all going. Life feels like one tight spot after another. Visibility is remarkably limited. Maybe we need to adjust our sights. Then again perhaps all we need to do is stay the course. I don't have answers, just recognizing how prevalent these moments of doubt are, whether we discuss them or push them away.

Less common is the discourse taken up by a group of fathers in the local Waldorf community. All very successful men in the world of business, they met for several months and grappled with one question: *How much money is enough?* To many people, this might sound absurd. But these men were sincere. All of them possessed that enviable Midas touch in business, yet they feared losing touch with their marriage, family, friends, health, personal goals, as well as the environment. Thus they contemplated: *How much is enough?* I appreciate and respect this contemplation.

Chapter 29 The Dual Nature of Money

It feels kind of strange to try to school anyone on the nature of money given the hundreds of everyday money moments involving cash, check, coin, plastic; involving that sneaky fast stream of money-infused thoughts and feelings; the many verbal interchanges with vendors, tellers, call centers, and the nonverbal nods and waves of the hand that say we're good for it. The message is ready-to-hand: Money moves through our world, everyone's world, even the world of the monk with the begging bowl. Therefore, it feels like we should know money, right? Of course we do, though we give ourselves considerable leverage the minute we recognize how money possesses a dual nature. *There is the money we make, and there is the money we then manage.* These are two distinctly different endeavors, with varying objectives, calling upon different skill sets. And while this insight is rather ordinary to the intellect, the real world application of it is far reaching. Might even save the day.

HEARTH MONEY V. HUNTER MONEY

In the course of our life we make money out in the world, at the office, on the road, on the phone, behind the counter, behind the wheel, maybe we work out of the home office: No matter—all of that pertains to Hunter Money. We may be the market maker, the minor league ball player, the master entertainer, the beloved schoolteacher, the biz dev rainmaker, the irrepressible barista who can out-quip each and every customer at the café counter, the Elephant Hunter who lands the big M&A deal, the poet who drives the cab through surreal American nights, the attorney who by day uses words like weapons. Again, I speak of the Hunter Money realm, where we interface with the world, ideally offering up some measure of value to our clients or the marketplace, for which we are remunerated.

Then we come home. Our paycheck gets deposited, cashed, or electronically wired into our personal bank account. Alchemical is this moment. What heretofore was "earned money" changes to "Hearth Money." With the money that now resides in the family purse, we pay the bills, go out to dinner, splurge for a fun outing, save some of our money, invest some, and so on. All that goes on there—the decisions about spending and saving, the strategies for investing, the actions and the non-actions of funding the retirement account, actually paying the bills, opening the statements, giving the kids money, tipping the bartender, buying the suede sport coat in San Francisco, purchasing a new horse, motorcycle, bike, what have you—all that transpires is Hearth Money. It's personal money.

Now things get curious. The two kinds of money are obviously interconnected. For example, what sense does it make to speak of personal money if we neither have nor earn any to begin with? The interconnection can also run the other way. How we manage (or mismanage) our personal financial affairs can make demands (appropriate or stressful) on our life as a hunter. All the time hasty business decisions are made because someone—professional, entrepreneur, investor—is under the gun on the personal money front. Money is owed to the taxman, big credit card bills are in need of payment, or there is the daily duress of white-knuckling one's way through an upper-middle class existence. But beyond these interconnections, they remain separate. The prescription for success with one kind of money doesn't necessarily fit with the other. That's the curious aspect. We may be the hunter extraordinaire out in the world; or, we may be the hunter who does all right, nothing more. But whatever that story is, it says not one word about how effective we will be in the realm of personal finance.

In a way this is NOT news. You and I know people—friends, neighbors, co-workers, family members—who have done well for themselves in business and yet somehow managed to underwhelm in the personal money department. They have less to show for their success than they should. But then we get thinking about it, and it's not always easy to locate the cause. The troubles of Paul the eminent psychologist, whom we visited amid his long fall to financial mediocrity, is case in point. Because he is an undeniably good chap and revered veteran clinician, it will set us to wondering: How can this be? What is lacking such that he would prove to be so misery-making with his family's personal money? Could it be education? No, he's got plenty of that. Common sense? No, by most all accounts he normally has his feet on the ground. Ability to make money? No, he's consistently an outstanding earner. Pedigree? No, he comes from good stock. Neurotic? Well, he's in the business of affliction-reduction, so he knows a thing or two about that. And yet there it is, a money affliction to beat the band. What gives?

In Paul's particular case there was a woeful lack of checks

and balances in the partnership. Had his wife Elisabeth engaged, surely he would have performed better. But how much better is very difficult to say, because some folks can receive reams of financial information and education, understand it all, yet in action still underwhelm. I believe some portion of this is attributable to a person's psycho-emotional hardwiring. It's how we tick in the personal money realm. Earlier we saw my nine-year-old nephew in action, wanting to negotiate a great deal at the holiday gift shop. He proudly returned with his purchase AND some change in his pocket. It meant a lot to him. Now in terms of my own relationship to personal money, I can't relate. Not remotely. But my wife can. She operates in a very similar fashion to my nephew. This has its benefits. When it's time to purchase a new family car, she goes into action. First she'll do her homework. All relevant car lots will be visited. Then she'll do some more homework. If the deal is real, she'll take it. If the deal is bogus, she'll be hard nosed. My money is on her that she'll come away with a sweet deal.

All in all it's a good thing that I get left out of such negotiations, because undoubtedly I'd be the weak link. Bargaining like this doesn't interest me. There's no juice in it for me. But now for the unexpected part: In terms of my business life, I have no issue at all in negotiating hard. In fact, I'm pretty perky about it. If my lease with my landlord is not compelling, I'll weigh my options and work it hard. That same tiger energy is available for my clients when they're in the throes of buying/selling a house, negotiating a deal or service, dealing with ginormous medical bills, or negotiating fees with outside professionals. But in my personal money life, no, I don't care that much. And this is illustrative of how not only is personal Hearth Money quite different than Hunter Money, but we ourselves literally boot up differently in each realm.

One of the best decisions I've made in my personal financial life was to relinquish singular control of the family purse, and rely on others whenever appropriate and feasible. Since then (I know I sound like The Converted, but it's true), life is better, business is better, and so are family finances. Now, I know there are plenty of folks, financial advisors among them, for whom personal money stuff is fun and sporting and a big part of how they occupy themselves away from the office. But that's not me. One kind of money really perks me up (Hunter Money). I love my work. I love helping my clients, and I thoroughly enjoy doing well for my firm. As for the other kind of money (Hearth Money), I'll do it as a part of a team. I'll adhere to the plan and the rules we make. I'll put in the required time, but not a second more.

In my first book, *Zen Money Blues,* I presented as foundational the notion that money has a dual nature. If you prefer more detailed thinking on the matter, by all means check out the book. Or, just try the idea on for size. Look at the world through this lens. Make the distinction between Hunter and Hearth Money. Observe in a fresh and penetrating way what in fact is taking place in the realm of Hearth Money—i.e., the personal financial realm of spending & saving, planning & implementing, investing, and decision making. The old way of looking at money in an undifferentiated manner has caused good folks to draw conclusions that were unwarranted and unhelpful. It's easy to do. It's also easy—with this little insight—to never do that again. But as we'll see, Bernard the Banker has yet to get the memo.

PORTRAIT OF A PLUMBER AND A BANKER

On the 7:09am train to Grand Central is Bernard the Banker, 38, bespectacled and impeccable in his bespoke suit. The guy looks like money, smells like money; his voice, though manly, even has the tinkle of gold and silver coins to it. Indisputable is that he's one of the hardest working young bankers at a reputable firm on Wall Street—a status he is reluctant to share after the banker- and politician-led financial meltdown of 2008. The stink on his profession is too bad because he is a stand-up guy, respected by his peers for doing deals properly, for generating value to his clients, as opposed to, say, pushing an acquisition through that is crap from the start. And for the most part Bernard has been paid nicely for his work. But let us be careful here: *Making money (i.e., being good at Hunter Money) neither confirms nor denies prowess in the realm of personal finances.* Furthermore, appearances (i.e., one's career in this case) may deceive. A guy in finance by day should excel at personal finances by night, if not do it in his sleep, right?

Forgive the stock characterizations, but let's play it the other way for a moment. Donny D. gets his butt out of bed at 3am on most days. He gives his neighbor, the bread baker, a ride downtown in his F-150 before he himself arrives at the garage. From 4:30 till 9:30 he'll haul garbage from alleyways and curbsides. Then from 9:30 to 3:00 he turns into indispensable handyman for any number of families with a punch list of stopped-up sinks, crooked cabinets, dysfunctional doorjambs, and the like. Glorious and celebrated his work life is not. Pay him the big bucks these activities won't. But Donny is quite the proficient one when it comes to managing his personal finances. For comparison purposes, "proficient" does not mean that Donny has to have the bigger house or drive the sweeter car than Bernard the Banker. Instead, the comparative measure is one of who's solid and in control versus who is not. Donny is in control, for sure. He owns the clothes on his back and the car in the driveway. His material life is honest. Synchronized. He's living within his means as a matter of course. Seldom is money a big worry.

Bernard, however, is far less proficient. To wit, he makes wads of cash here and there, and covers a wide array of commitments. Periodically, though, he has acute bouts of feeling out of control with his Hearth Money. That flipping back and forth between loving his luscious life and resenting it, even in moments feeling anxiety-riddled about it, is stressful. Bernard is not alone. There are accountants, attorneys, academics, executives, and so on—the well dressed, the highly educated—who share Bernard's experience. They expect to be as good in handling their Hearth Money as they are at making money. But experience doesn't bear this out. Some of these folks may be just plain too busy. Some of them, however, may have expectations of themselves that are highly unrealistic. Maybe we find Bernard isn't very good at planning, implementing, investing—not by himself anyway. So what! Really, we'd rather know that truth than be lost like Bernard. Then we can arrange accordingly. But we won't see any of this if we don't first discern the two kinds of money, and who we are in each of those realms.

Chapter 30 Old News

By making the Hunter/Hearth money distinction, we can see more sharply the field of play. Personal money is its own game. It has its own rules and objectives that pertain to saving & spending, planning & implementing, investing, and decision making. HR decisions for personal money are different from HR decisions at the firm. There's no room for inflated egos or lazy assumptions. We want to know who is good at what, and place them in positions and activities that play to their strengths. If we need outside help to fill certain gaps, we get outside help. No more fuzzy view of money. No more fizzy intoxication with business experience and education credentials that augur next to nothing about one's personal money effectiveness. Now we can organize our personal money world much more effectively.

By making the Hunter/Hearth distinction, we can also save ourselves (or someone we love) from an otherwise avoidable world of pain. I don't wish to outline rulebooks on the two kinds of money and how they act and interact, but the following illustrations serve as reminders to not freely and easily mix them. I think you'll see what I mean. First up is Lenny. He's in a very bad way. He has made an unfortunate error, one that could cost him and his family everything. Adding insult to financial injury, the matter is fodder for the popular press. After him comes Annie L. Ultimately she will elude great harm, but not without first being the talk of the town.

NAILS

From the not too distant past you may recall Lenny Dykstra. He played centerfield for the New York Mets, where his nickname was "Nails," as in "Tough as Nails." And seemingly he was. He was a kind of modern day Ty Cobb, much beloved by the hometown. But retirement wasn't kind to Lenny. No, I don't know the guy personally, just read about him in *Yahoo! Sports* one recent summer's morning when I should have been working. The long and short of that story: Lenny's broke. For all the bones he made back in the day playing ball, he's plumb broke now and owes another $40M to the brokerage firms who lent him capital. Apparently, Lenny put all his money (approx. $12M) into his investment/hedge fund business venture, personally secured additional loans from banks and brokerage firms, lost it all, and now finds himself in bankruptcy court.

By the by, Lenny Dykstra's error wasn't that his hedge fund business went under. Business ventures crash all the time. You can have the best concept, the best management team, the best plan, decent capital, and still ventures crash for untold, unanticipated reasons. Sometimes it really is no one's fault, a case of bad luck. Why Lenny's hedge fund went under, I know not. But the egregious error, to my mind, occurred the moment Lenny put all his assets (personal) into the game (business). You don't empty the kitchen cupboard to feed a business venture. You don't mix the two kinds of money as recklessly and easily as he seemingly did. Business ventures, as noted, fail all the time. Since that is a very real outcome for any one of us, no matter how smart or seasoned we are, it is prudent to also think through the possible scenario of failure and its impact on the family purse. This is not pessimism. This is reality. Our personal financial planning therefore takes all the possible outcomes into account. Proper attention is paid to both kinds of money, and how they interrelate. Lenny Dykstra missed this, or so it appears. I shudder to think of the possible fallout to him and his family.

PHOTOS BY ANNIE L.

A covey of women, no doubt, have their own rendition of Lenny "Nails" Dykstra, of Paul the psychotherapist, of Sir Winston, and—if you've read *Zen Money Blues*—of the lovable but financial house afire character, Mr. Broccoli Raab. Women are not immune to the desires and confusion around money and self-identity, around keeping score on a material and psychological plane, around asserting their prowess as hunters and wealth generators, around parading their wealth, though it does seem less common that we read about women who made it and then, because of their wild expansive ideas or massive ego, blew it all. The stories must be there, and are surely worth searching for.

Now that said, not long after I wrote this, the finances of Annie Leibovitz were unflatteringly spread across the front page of the *New York Times* online edition. It seems that she'd borrowed a pile of cash from a New York boutique lending firm, to invest in real estate, and she pledged as collateral the rights to the portfolio of her extraordinary life's work as a photographer. *Her life's work.* This could not go to a good place. Indeed, the *New York Times* article was reading that made for wincing. It was photo without a fig leaf, pain without a pill. Sometime before the economic disaster of 2008, Annie had had an idea and it went something like this. *Manhattan real estate: How can it miss? Bet the house, bet the farm, er, bet my life's work. I love this idea. I'm all in.* Wrathfully, the Recession smote her can't-miss real estate play. The time of loan-default fast approached; hence, the article. Based on the reader comments, people were aghast at the implications. It did feel weird to think that her life's work could go to some downtown clowns in business suits.

After a while the whole matter shifted in my mind, however. In the distance I could hear the Zen Money chorus, singing sweetly from the heavens, and I found myself thinking: "Annie, Annie, Annie—your life's work possibly ending up in a pawn shop? Come on over here. We gotta talk ... with love, mind you ... but we gotta talk."

. . . .

Why we make severe financial misjudgments and then take action on them is obviously a terribly complex affair. Individual maturity and emotional intelligence doubtless factor in. So too does the presence or absence of checks and balances. Experiences, and what we glean from them, weigh heavily. Quality of counsel and information clearly matter. How disciplined our decision-making process is or is not (i.e., good planning, good thought partners), matters. Luck or lack thereof ever figures in, or so the great statisticians of our time tell us. Our psychological inclination toward under/over-confidence matters, as per the 2001 MIT study. Psychological hang-ups sometimes matter. Now do allow room for one more causal agent; an agent broached earlier, an agent that I believe is easily overlooked, yet proves to be a major player: Our cognitive/emotional wiring. It was implied (rather parodically) in the Tightwad and Spendthrift study, and was a hub of investigation in *Zen Money Blues*. Although it has been a few years since penning that work, I still hold to the view that there is a psychic substratum for each one of us that is not changeable. Fixed. It's just who we are, and gets activated the moment we enter the realm of personal money, aka Hearth Money. It's there when we spend or save. It's there when we receive (or reject) the counsel of others. We don't need the CPA to tell us to put 5K in the IRA this year, we know that; but will we? Perhaps we do need the CPA to tell us to do this, because although we "know" we should do it, we rarely think to do it.

But this is neither the time nor place for a recapitulation of the Typology espoused in *Zen Money Blues*. For one, sound bites are the bane of modern cultural discourse. Let's not go there. For two, we don't necessarily need the ZM Types to get a good look at the prime mover of personal finance; namely, our hard to see, but always acting financial self. The ZM Types provide one kind of looking glass, reflecting back the lively archetypal characters who inhabit the personal money realm. In Lion Hearted Love, we have taken a similar, albeit more process-oriented tack. We can be keen in our observations, first in regards to the proverbial Other Guy, then in regards to our own track record of actions, emotions, and effectiveness. *Let's go Open Book in the partnership of love, money, economy, and relationship.* It's gritty. It's efficacious. It might even become cheerful.

POST-AMBLE

Chapter 31 Open Road

I hope I have not overstated money's place. Of course, money engenders all manner of opposites: fun and trouble, pride and anxiety, unity and discord, excitement and ennui. But marriages end up on the rocks for a bevy of reasons. Money may not figure in at all. Or, it may play the lead. Other times it will be a part of the supporting cast. Just depends. Ditto on the family front. Relations between and across generations may get strained. The role money plays may really be beside the point. In another scene it may be central. Therefore, the disclaimer: Just because the focus of *Lion Hearted Love* is on money-in-relationship, this work is in no way an attempt to assert some larger universal claim about the root of all marital and family woes. If only! Grandpa Bill had an ego the size of Alaska and the repercussions of that extended into the nooks, closets, and private rooms of their marriage, places that had nothing whatsoever to do with money. Money is rarely the whole story, but it is a character that surely seems to appear in a lot of episodes.

Perhaps you have seen the sublime Gabriel Byrne in the HBO series, *In Treatment*, speaking of episodes. Intense. In an early episode of the first season, Byrne—the intrepid, skilled, and generally compassionate psychotherapist (who has a truly worrisome blind spot of his own)—is working with a client, a medical doctor named Laura. During the session she communicates how fed up she is with the groveling of her boyfriend, as he continues to desperately press her to make a real commitment to the relationship: *In or out?* Laura sees his maneuvers as flat-out manipulation. This is not surprising. Laura is a tiger, viewing marriage as code for captivity. To complicate matters, she's also a tiger who's madly in love with her therapist. But I'm getting ahead of myself. In the course of their dialogue Byrne, the therapist, inquires as to why Laura sees her guy's tears as pathetic and manipulative. With a bright schadenfreude smile, she replies: "Don't you know that men are the new women?"

Ah, gender, with its once established but now defunct rules, roles, and expectations. That pillbox of prescriptions was emptied out with the Death of Certainty. Even so, gender colors and tints how we see our self and others, and has a knack for shaping the story of money in our private life. It is no state secret that men are still prone to an inflated sense of their financial prowess while women are prone to deflation. The residue doesn't end there. How many women—apropos personal finances—put up with an erratic husband rather than take him on for fear of emasculating him around money? I don't know, but echoes of this are certainly out there. What about the higher divorce rate for marriages where the woman is making the big bucks?[20] What's that about? It's not 1970 and it's definitely not 1950.

The topic of gender—with money and career firing its twin turbo engines—remains evocative and at times volatile. Mainstream publishers are onto this, presently promoting pseudo-expert books wrapped in sound-bite titles such as, *The End of*

Men. While such projects are fantastic for grabbing attention and selling books, they're obviously lowbrow attempts to fan the flames, if not out-and-out throw gasoline on the fire. I imagine others also perceive these books and articles as just plain goofy. Either way, the present time is not characterized by the battle of the sexes. It's big-boy / big-girl rules out there. People from different walks of life are making some interesting and rather diverse choices. And it's on this note that I'd like to bring *Lion Hearted Love* to a close with a few final observations mingled with a few aspirations.

THE TIMES

Lion Hearted Love is a story of how we might rise to the occasion of freedom and prosperity in the time after Certainty died. Winston and Clementine Churchill lived in the time of Certainty. That worked both for them and against them. Winston never questioned his place in their financial world, and that wreaked stress and havoc on them. Clemmie questioned *his place* in their financial world, but would never have clout to do anything about it till after Winston died. Had they lived in these past 40 years, I imagine fabulous rows, fabulous heavyweight championship fights of their household, and my money would most definitely be on Clemmie. But I'm getting carried away.

For our children, for our nieces and nephews, and for our best friend's kids—the time of Uncertainty is normal to them. The freedoms unleashed are also normal. I think this represents real progress, chaos notwithstanding, education not overlooked. Today it is no longer considered outlandish for any one of us to periodically take the time in our life to try to figure out who we are and what we want. Today there are fewer curmudgeons who make scathing remarks about a man or a woman deviating from "traditional" gender roles, though of course they are still out there. All in all, it's a different world and the stigma attached to not following a deeply grooved track or becoming a company man is less prevalent. Besides, with the demolition of the economy in 2008, the so-called traditional tracks aren't looking too functional anyway.

Meantime, the waves of demographic facts keep rolling in. As compared to 1970, it's a veritable sea change. America now has more women in the work force than men.[21] In heterosexual marriage, women are more educated than the guys.[22] This is not a surprise after perusing college enrollment data from the year 2000 onward. Colleges on average are matriculating 56% women vs. 44% men. In private small colleges the spread is closer to 60%/40%.[23] No doubt many young women are going for it. Pulling themselves up by the proverbial bootstraps. Clearly, too, there is another trend: Americans are investing in their daughters! And, finally, the marrying stats are not subtle. Although Americans remain the most marrying people on the planet, the institution of marriage is conspicuously on the decline. The biggest drop is among the less educated and lower income earners. The college educated, by contrast, continue to marry at a robust rate (about 68% of young people), though that still represents a decline from the 1970's rate of 82%.[24]

True to our earlier social psychology note about "birds of a feather," the college educated do tend to marry other college educated people. Although the data are far from conclusive, a college education does seem to stand out as a stabilizing factor in marriage—i.e., showing significantly lower divorce rates than the less educated. What's that about? The obvious is economic. The more educated you are, the more earnings power you have. Contributing economically—overtly or potentially—reinforces the notion of equality in the marital partnership. And, whether in a robust or a funky economy, the college educated do much better (job-wise) than those without a degree. In addition to economy, higher education serves a vital psychological component. At its best it encourages the young people to be individuals, to think for themselves, to act as they see fit—in a phrase, to be their own person. I think it axiomatic that a healthy sense of self pays huge dividends in relationship, particularly in these modern times when roles and responsibilities are periodically negotiated.

THE OTHER EDUCATION

Emotional intelligence is the less obvious, though arguably most critical 21st-century course of study. If you're lucky, your spouse will already have emotional intelligence in spades, because nothing works without it. For all the notions espoused in *Lion Hearted Love*—from Kula wisdom to smartly putting the right players in the right positions, from taking note of the brass tacks of money to relaxing ego—none of it will work without this cornerstone of character. For example, emotional intelligence is at work when we lightly deflate our ego. *All right, I'm lost. Time to ask for directions.* It's there when we motivate ourselves to do the scut work—i.e., of budgeting—that we'd really rather not do. *I loathe budgeting. Really and truly. Makes me feel like a kid. But not doing it is insanity. Ergo, we'll work the budget.* It's there when we feel that prick of hesitation, when we question our assumed acumen on a specific financial matter or judgment, pushing us to seek the counsel or thought partnership of another. *Maybe I know less about Apple stock than I thought. Hmmm. Maybe I'm being driven by greed, not objective, patient analysis.*

Emotional intelligence is the fruit of developing not just the thinking side of the mind, but the emotional/feeling side, too.

Then thought and feeling can work more effectively together. *I thought buying the BMW was a "must have." Upon reflection, I admit it's really a want. And I do want it. But...* There's nothing wrong with being passionate about what we want, but it needs to be recognized and counterbalanced. It isn't possible to effectively manage passion and/or impulse if we don't even know we are in the throes of it! In this way, the notion of emotional intelligence is considerably more dynamic than, say, the term maturity. The latter too often has a moral tone. As well, it doesn't account for the fact that emotions often lie in our blind spot, influencing decisions and actions unbeknownst to us.

Emotional intelligence is white hot in executive leadership coaching circles right now. On more than one occassion, I've heard executive coaches assert that an alarmingly high percentage of global corporate executives don't know how they feel in the moment,[25] which is to say, they're unconscious of their emotions much of the time. Think about that! An executive may be deeply worried about a particular issue, yet say he's fine with things. Meanwhile, all his people already pick up on the vibe that things are in a bad way. Whatever he says, the words sure as heck aren't going to mean a whole lot to his crew. One can see all the looks being shot around the room by the staff behind his back. So much for leadership! So much for problem solving! By contrast, the leader who 1) knows how he feels about an issue (*I'm very concerned*), 2) can process his emotions (*Okay, I'm intimidated, but at the same time we can make a plan to give us a fighting chance at success*), and 3) accordingly communicates to his staff with bandwidth of thought and feeling—that leader will come off as credible and genuine. Success is not assured, but neither is there the predictable mutiny from the get-go.

Fearlessness in the Shambhala tradition draws from the same source. No doubt, it is intimidating for us to cede some control in relationship, to relax ego, to go Open Book in regards to our strengths and weaknesses, and to maybe not be as awesome in every life scene as we'd like to be. But fearlessness doesn't mean we block the emotions. Nor do we drown in them. Rather we seek the middle, where even though we feel awkward, insecure, or vulnerable, we nevertheless rouse our best self. And that makes all the difference. This mode of emotional intelligence is part and parcel of how we get rich from experience, learning from victories and mistakes alike, as opposed to ignoring the data points and lessons that our financial life will surely serve up.

Chapter 32 Circle Back

Throughout much of the second half of *Lion Hearted Love*, I have agitated for marital partnerships to go Open Book. This is to say: By dispassionately observing and sharing information about who is good at what (and who is middling at what), the partners could more effectively organize and work together in financial matters. But that presupposed each of the players was already in the game. This, we know, is not always the case. For a million different reasons the control of family finances is still often dominated by one spouse. If the marriage is good, this is a lost opportunity. If the marriage is unstable, this is dangerous. In a progressive and highly educated town like Boulder, I am somewhat surprised at how many couples have one spouse, usually the woman, who is unengaged. A colleague and I have discussed this phenomenon at length, and her take is that many of these women (with their children now older) would like to engage, but they've been out of the family financial loop for a long time and thus feel at a bit of a loss as to where to begin or what to even ask, for fear of looking stupid.

My counsel here is very simple, whether the marriage is on firm ground, or not: Engage. Then take on some responsibilities, try some things out. It is imperative to find out what kind of game you have, right now. Find out for you, find out for the partnership. Too bad my dad never knew what kind of partner he had in my mom. Even after he lost the Heavyweight Championship of our house in 1971, thereby changing some of the roles and responsibilities of their partnership, there was no challenge posed to purse control. But then life happened. Then Mom got put to the test.

Untested, Then Tested

Rye, New York (1972) – Early evenings in summer were like this. Orange sun slowly sank behind the red brick of Milton Elementary School. Gulls from the harbor headed home. Upstairs in our house, before that brightly lit mirror, sat Mom in girdle and bra. The room pixillated with the smell of hairspray. Dad came home and changed into his white shoes. That meant *party*. Down the hall Grandma's bedroom door was open. She listened to the black-and-white TV while she knitted. In the evening she was always knitting or working at the sewing machine. Tonight she'd also keep an ear out for us kids.

In autumn, there was a clutch of parties at Republican headquarters. We kids got to go to those parties. Hence, we liked politics! Conservative "Grand Old Party" in name, the NY Rockefeller Republicans rocked it hard when it came to party time. *Bash* was the word, and bash it was. Even as primary school kids, we knew a good bash when it was upon us, and election night and the post-caucus parties had us staying up way past our bedtime. And Mom, well, she was seriously annoyed, which added to the delight and specialness.

Then there were the holiday parties, many of which were at our house. One particular holiday fête still blazes vividly in my mind, roaring well into the night. In fact, it crackled and roared so loud and so long that I, a lad of 10, could not sleep a wink, and after listening to the party guests shriek and talk-yell at each other in a crescendo that was reaching a fevered pitch, I snuck partway downstairs to the landing to examine for myself what was so dang fun. And, well, it was mind-stopping.

Bottles of booze and highball glasses and ashtrays everywhere, and a haze of smoke permeated the room; but that was normal. What wasn't normal was the dancing; or, more precisely, the dancers' getups. Mom, Dad—my parents—and their upstanding friends—Mr. Bonn and Mrs. Bonn, and Mr. Fox and Mrs. Fox, and Mr. Stenholm and Mrs. Stenholm, and Mr. Green and Mrs. Green—were dancing in their skivvies. No two ways about it. Girdles and bras and boxer shorts, and shoulders and legs and belly buttons and hairy chests; and everyone was grinning, and their eyes were flashing, and the dancing (Credence Clearwater Revival was on the turntable) wasn't very good, so much so that I feared that someone was bound to dance right into the Christmas tree and take it down, Angel of Mercy and all; and I wished I'd stayed in bed. Utterly perplexed at the goings on, I finally decided I was sleepwalking—which everyone in my family was always accusing me of doing anyway—and headed back to my room, to my bed, and fell fast asleep, while downstairs the fires raged and the band played on.

And then it was over.

Not just the party. All of it.

It's like in Bergman's final film, *Fanny and Alexander*, where the children seemingly live this family life amid velvet and brass and burnished candle glow, and there is the riot of family and holidays and love and aunts and uncles and cousins and grandparents, and then suddenly it's over. The father dies. A certain austere reality casts its pall. And that's what happened. About a month before President Richard M. Nixon resigned from the Oval Office, amidst a vicious economic recession, my father left this world after a brief and aggressive sickness, and my mother, Karen, once a white-glove wearing graduate of Penn Hall finishing school, and more recently matriculated in the bachelors of fine arts program at Manhattanville College, was now in charge of the kingdom. She was scared, as were we all.

The expression "Over my dead body" took on its own awful visceral meaning then. No one knew it also had its ray of hope. Mom, widowed at the age of 36, formally prepared not one iota to deal with the money of hunt or hearth, all her adult life a homemaker in the 1950's style, now had a brimming-over "life portfolio." For starters, there were three grocery stores to be run. In 1974, the grocery business was—unmistakably—a man's business. Sure, women's lib was doing its thing, but much of it was still symbolic, like Billy Jean King whooping Bobby Riggs's butt on the tennis court. It was nice and all, a definite feel-good, but the butchers, the vendors, the guys who made the store run—well, it was a cash business, a man's business, and if you did not watch yourself, you could find your livelihood had gone out the back door by dint of the nickel-and-dime, everyday petty thievery that occurred in a business of tangible hard goods and cash. How to bust balls, how to bust chops, how to make heads roll—how to get through and be taken seriously in a man's business, Mom got a crash course on that. Failure was not an option. Four kids and a home and all that she and Dad had built—losing that or falling backwards just simply wasn't an option. Fortunately, Mom was a quick study in the realm of Hunter Money. Who knew?

Time wills out that Mom was also stellar in the personal money realm. This was a surprise, as well. While she may have won the 1971 Heavyweight Championship of our household, that fight did not include personal finances. Although it was an historical time of great flux, I'm not sure she could have won that fight. Not for a long time, anyway. But Dad's passing made that moot. In a shocking sink-or-swim moment, Mom was put to the test. Her instinctive response had her learning from everyone and everything, errors included.

With the big stuff, so with the small stuff, she was excellent. She was the prototypical squirrel-awayer of money. She did this for everything: for college for four kids, for an apartment for Grandma Millie, even for vacations to the Caribbean. Traditional IRA's were first legislated back in the '70's; there wasn't a year that Mom failed to contribute. In a time when women were hardly the poster-child for much of anything beyond the 1950's prototype, Mom met her moment of truth with elegance, grit, and a bit of luck.

As in any family, of course, there were miscalculations and imperfections and grumblings and grievances. There also were more than a few white-knuckle moments along the way; and I would be remiss to not recognize that Grandma Millie was stalwart and that we four kids, a few adolescent blips notwithstanding, repeatedly rose to the occasion. Still and all, amidst the very nasty economic environment of the mid-1970's, Mom got it done. She had the right stuff, and she ultimately put it to good use. But what if Dad had never died? Would she have discovered her array of talents? I wonder.

. . . .

In this day and age, divorce, much more than widowhood, is the event that frequently puts a woman on the spot. Financial advisors can't miss this trend. Women find themselves on their own and they seek education, thought partnership, more education, and someone to light-handedly help them be accountable to themselves. As for those who feel they have a solid and trustworthy marriage, perhaps a marriage of many years, I have to say quite directly: *Don't be comfortable if you are the Untested.* Starting right now, put yourself to the test (lovingly and kindly, of course). Give various aspects of personal finance a go. Whether you meet with success or make mistakes, in all cases become a keen student of the game. Never sell yourself short. You may discover you have great instincts for any number of financial matters. Then again, maybe not! Either way you now will truly be Open Book in your marital partnership. This is good. It's good to know what kind of game you've got. Who knows what tomorrow may bring?

Speaking of the future, this initiation most definitely applies to the young people. This is a topic I hope to broach in a subsequent work. But, now, a few words on this intergenerational matter. As the young people in our world come of age, we should repeatedly put them to the test, and discuss the results with them each time. They, like us, need to learn by experience. Along the way, though, let's serve as thought partner and light-handed guide. I'm confident the 20-somethings in our world are willing to be engaged on this level. Let's then engage them. The road to financial mediocrity is paved with lessons unlearned. What a waste. Money no longer needs to be so taboo. Victories are worth contemplating and discussing. So are defeats. And, even after the young people find the love of their life, there is still much to be discussed. The young people need thought partners just the same. However, if this dialogue feels too emotionally charged or enmeshed, thereby disqualifying any one of us from serving in the role of helper, surely there is a family friend or aunt or uncle or grandparent who can step up and help. Such friends are often just waiting to be summoned, or so I'd like to believe.

Chapter 33 The Gift, Full Dazzling

We began our journey with an exploration of the gift economy, and within that, the Kula of Marriage; and we conclude our journey accordingly, drinking from the cup of *the gift* one final time, care of my flamboyant artist brother, John, who was 19 at the time. The occasion was always the unveiling of John's latest works of art, and the venue was usually my mother's house. Family and friends reliably rallied for these teatime parties, and for us as a family, as survivors of our father's early departure from this world, these were the times of sweetness and mischief and mirth. Mom would bustle round the house beforehand, taking down and hiding the risqué paintings that Grandma Millie would not approve of. John would quietly put one or two or three back up—just to keep it real. Indeed, these were great family times together. Somehow, we were blessed to know that such good fortune was upon us while it was happening. Which brings us to our closing anecdote on the gift, care of my Whitman-esque brother.

LITHOGRAPHS
Not everyone shared my brother John's idea of economy. It

made Grandma Millie terribly nervous. The year was 1983. Mention the year, and John would recite Hendrix: " ... a merman I should turn to be," though at that point John was much more inclined to the artful, political edginess of the Clash and Joe Strummer. His Doc Martens boots and epauletted army surplus coats and shrieking hair reflected this. In terms of his own art, John was on a pen and ink jag, and was often found working on long sheets of industrial brown paper. Intermittently, he worked on a series of outsized oil-based paintings on driftwood and other wrack and spawn from the waters of Long Island Sound; and, as ever, the nudes. The latter marked his return to sports, albeit in the mode of artist. It was John playing in centerfield all over again, studying anthills while the little league game was being played, waving at teenagers in derelict cars passing by, squinting into the rays of the sun that slid through the webbing of his baseball mitt—except now, ten years later, the game was football on canvas.

John was enchanted by America's other beloved pastime. Before long he'd convey that enchantment into a riot of art pieces, showing us the game through his looking glass. Now, imagine a Sunday afternoon in fall, your favorite football team on the telly. The players lumber up to the line of scrimmage, and assume their stance for the big play. You yourself have been lying on the couch, perhaps exhausted from too much work in the yard or from a monster week at the office, and heroically you rouse; you sit up to watch the big play, lean into the action, while religiously and continuously dipping fingers into the popcorn bowl. However, there's a John Butler-imposed change of cameras. Every athlete on the field of battle is now *sans* equipment, *sans* uniform. Indeed, each is nude and natural as Michelangelo's David. Ripped muscles and round buttocks and family jewels abound. *Goddammit! Is nothing sacred?*, you might scream, neither amused nor taken by this display of the male anatomy in its prime. That disruption would please John. Popcorn taking flight would be even better. But I digress.

The season was in fact fall, and there we were, close friends and family, assembled at my mother's house to view John's newest work. As he was in a prolific phase of art creation, this type of gathering seemed to occur every few weeks. Pen and ink comprised the latest piece, perhaps 3' by 5'. The drawing had that graffiti-effect phenomenon. You had to stay with it till slivers of order emerged from the chaos. Accordingly, we huddled around and gazed at it for an uncomfortably long time.

Attending that afternoon fête was John's partner, Allyn. An English professor at one of the local colleges, Allyn was doing his level best to not burst into song regarding John's latest piece. Indeed, he trilled not. The moment was John's. The young artist himself was effusive, employing a breathless, early Bob Dylan syntax, providing rangy explanations that explained nothing any of us could follow. But who cared! It was a share the moment thing; enjoy the art and John's colorful verbal fills. It was John and it was fun. It was definitely fun.

But fun is not for everyone.

"Lithographs," Grandma Millie said, breaking ranks. "John, you should think about lithographs. That's the way to go."

This, of course, was our American Grandmother who worked 8am to 4pm, 50 weeks per year, in the basement of a grocery store, our grocery store, impeccably managing the books for the food business and our family's burgeoning commercial real estate business. Perhaps not the warmest grandmother in all of christendom, she nonetheless was very fond of John. Always had been.

John had a hard-to-read look on his face.

"That Roy Lichtenstein recently did it," Grandma went on,

offering what perhaps she saw as the missing and much needed business model. "I read it in the *New York Post*. One thousand signed lithographs at $350 apiece. Leroy Neiman did it, too, though I'm not a fan of his work. Too splashy for my taste."

"Lithographs," John said, carefully. "I'll keep that in mind, Grandma."

Grandma relaxed after that. John kept her close, kindly putting his arm around her for the entire teatime hour, while he visited with each and every one of us. This was just like John. He knew Grandma was a worrier *nonpareil*. And we all knew why Grandma worried. It came of the Great Depression and later from being jilted by Grandpa. Her world had been rocked, and not in the way young folks turn that phrase today. Getting financially ahead would never in this lifetime be hers, even if she never again took a sick day, even if she really was tough as Lou Gehrig (and way tougher than Lenny "Nails" Dykstra). Nor would Grandma in the afternoon of life ever get to take her fair share of victory laps.

This is where we grandchildren came in. She expected us to accomplish what eluded her. As commonplace as this might sound, she meant it. Grandma wasn't working in the basement for nothing. John's art was nice and all—"I don't get it, but that doesn't stop rich people from buying it," she said—but all Grandma could see was a valuable pen and ink commodity hanging on the wall. Leverage it, and make something of yourself. That was her mono-thesis. That was Grandma's wish.

Now did that business wish extend to John's sporting nudes? It's hard to say, because Mom hid them away best as she could whenever Grandma came over to the house. Regarding notions of art and economy and scalability, John was not to be dissuaded. Not then, not since. His art was his art. It wasn't for sale. It was a gift from the muses and he treated it thus. As for looking after

Grandma that afternoon, John was one long charm offensive. He could make Grandma laugh, and laugh she did. He could make her forget, and for the moment, forget she did. Even about the lithographs.

· · · · · · · · ·

For the last 2500-plus years it has been the Artist who has been the gift's Great Defender in the Western world. This is the Artist as Hero. Incorruptible. Profit cannot persuade him to abandon his artistic vision, though doubtless in spots he will employ guile. He must serve his Muse, his Genius, above all else, while simultaneously figuring out how to put food in his belly; or, so the story goes. It is not an easy arrangement. Nevertheless, the Artist as Hero is a widely admired character, a romantic figure, especially among the young; and, rightly so. He is his own man. He cannot be bought or sold. Whether the world recognizes his genius is not his main concern. It'd be nice, but "success" doesn't hinge on it. Just ask my brother John, who all his life has walked the way of the Artist.

Not everyone is a priest for his/her art like John, we know. Plenty of artists go the commercial route. For them, art is a commodity to be exploited. Lofty notions of gift property are regarded as ivory tower. Theirs is a business of entertainment, or a business of celebrity, with a smidge of art mixed in. Of course there are countless variations between pure art and pure commercialism. Some of it is done very tastefully. Here, as before, we see the natural interplay of capital and the gift.

· · · · · · · · ·

As we head for home, I'd like us to hold in mind the delightful and strange idea that gift property has—to use Lewis Hyde's words—an *erotic* life. In the authentic gift economy, such property is less about gratifying ego and more about connecting couples, families, clans, tribes, communities, and societies. *Wealth and property are subordinate to, and in the service of relationship.* It is the erotic element that was protected by the ancient rules of the gift circle: 1) The gift moves, and 2) The gift property is to remain gift property. Without these social rules, the gift would have been forever vulnerable to plunder and perversion. Without them, the unifying magic of gift property would have been lost, resulting in bankrupt relationships.

In our modern American world, where the acculturating bias is toward success in the capital sense, many of us have long been intuitively aware of this other counterbalancing economy, the gift, yet have been at a loss for how to articulate it, how to bring it to the fore. Where there is love and partnership, what's really going on? How can love and relationship be enriched, and not depleted, by the good material fortune that many of us experience? What's really going on in the give-and-take that is marriage? How can we account for that high-bandwidth mix of both material and psychological offerings? Like the preindustrial Melanesians of New Guinea, we'd like to stave off relationship bankruptcy. Like them, we'd like to be relationship-rich. But in our case, it doesn't stop there. Our material objectives are also included. They may be large, modest, or small. In all instances, we'd like to do the practical side of money exceedingly well. Actually, it's imperative that we do the practical side of money well.

Relationship, at least how we're visualizing relationship in *Lion Hearted Love*, can certainly be its own kind of art. Our everyday life serves as the canvas. And, like that stash of my brother John's paintings, it includes its fair share of nudity. Love reveals us. Love revealed Sir Winston. He had a less than sublime performance at lunch, and nearly got his head handed to him by Lady Clemmie. But time and again, love also laid bare his big heart. He loved Clemmie. She in turn loved him. Even so, none of this was easy. Nor is it today. Knowing when to yield, when to support, when to stake our claim, when to change it up—that is so nuanced and situational and evolving. There's no science for that. Nor is there some lingering culturally correct set of answers. Instead, today, there is dialogue. There is trial and error. There is creativity and revision. There is discipline and bravery. The Modern Kula of Marriage isn't some new set of answers. That won't work. Rather it's an artful way of seeing and thinking and conversing about the myriad details and the big arcs of the relationship—love included, money included. Then we have the best possible chance for partnership victory. Then we have the best possible chance for relationship peace. V for victory. V for peace. Onward!

1. *National Center for Health Statistics.* Note: These stats refer to the "Crude Divorce Rate," so named because it identifies the number of people per one thousand who get divorced in a given year in America. The conspicuous problem with this method of measurement is that this sample pool includes children as well as adults who may have no interest in marriage. Moreover, the reported numbers since 1996 don't include all of the American population, as this is a state-by-state compilation, and not all states report their divorce data to the National Center for Health Statistics.

According to a 2005 article, "Divorce Rate: It's Not As High As You Think," by Dan Hurley of the *New York Times*, "the method preferred by social scientists in determining the divorce rate is to calculate how many people who have ever married subsequently divorced. Counted that way, the rate has never exceeded about 41 percent, researchers say. Although sharply rising rates in the 1970's led some to project that the number would keep increasing, the rate has instead begun to inch downward." Now, while this is a tidy approach, it excludes folks who get married more than once from the rate—as if their subsequent marriages literally don't count. I think that's a big oversight.

In sum, the crude divorce rate is understandably far from beloved, but there really isn't any other longitudinal statistic out there. So, we'll go with it and call it good enough. And as for my comments about the incidence of divorce peeking in the early 1980's, here is what Hurley said: "What all experts do agree on is that, after more than a century of rising divorce rates in the United States, the rates abruptly stopped going up around 1980."

2. As discussed above: Divorce rate statistics are unsatisfying! What we really want to know from them is what's going on! Who's hanging together and who isn't, and of course, why. But there are emerging trends. Some were cited in Hurley's 2005 article, and have since been elaborated on in studies by the Pew Center for Social Research on the topic of marriage and divorce (see the 122-page report at: *http://www.pewsocialtrends.org/2010/11/18/ the-decline-of-marriage-and-rise-of-new-families/*). In a nutshell, here's what's emerging: Fewer people are getting married. Those who do are waiting longer. For a variety of reasons, some of which I hit on in this book, higher education (i.e., college) is a stabilizing marital force. The latter trend is corroborated by the quantifiably reduced rate of divorce occurring in the first 10 years of marriage among the educated. The non-college educated as a group is marrying less than the college educated.

3. David Watson, Eva C. Klohnen, Alex Casillas, Ericka N. Simms, Jeffrey Haig, and Diane S. Berry (2004), "Match Makers and Deal Breakers: Analyses of Assortative Mating in Newlywed Couples," *Journal of Personality*, 72 (5), 1029-68.

4. Lewis Hyde, *The Gift: Imagination and the Erotic Life of Property* (New York: Random House Vintage Books, 1983), p. 13.

5. Stephanie Pappas, "Love of Money May Mess Up Your Marriage;" *LiveScience*; October 13, 2011. Study cited in this article: "Materialism and Marriage: Couple Profiles of Congruent and Incongruent Spouses," by J.S. Carroll, L.R. Dean, L. Larson, and D.M. Busby (2011); *Journal of Couple and Relationship Therapy*, 10, 287-308.

Also of interest, an article on Harvard professor of psychology Daniel Gilbert: Chuck Leddy, "Money, Marriage, Kids;" *Harvard Gazette*, February 21, 2013; *http://news.harvard.edu/gazette/*

story/2013/02/money-marriage-kids/.

6. William Manchester, *The Last Lion: Alone 1932-1940* (London: Little, Brown and Company, 1988), p. 260. Quotation sourced from the Churchill Archives Centre, Churchill College, Cambridge.

7. Chögyam Trungpa, *Shambhala: The Sacred Path of the Warrior* (Boston & London: Shambhala Publications, 1984). Shambhala finds expression in the West in both secular and Buddhist forms. The above book is based on Trungpa Rinpoche's mind *terma*. The Shambhala teachings are rooted in the Kalachakra tantra and Tibetan lore.

8. A May 2007 article from Ohio State research scientist, Dr. Jay Zagorsky, examines the intelligence of individuals and how that affects both their personal financial management and their income. Intelligence—and its corresponding education—is king when it comes to income. This makes sense. According to a report on the study at *http://researchnews.osu.edu/archive/intlwlth. htm*, "the average income difference between a person with an IQ score in the normal range (100) and someone in the top 2 percent of society (130) is currently between $6000 and $18,500 a year. But when it came to total wealth and the likelihood of financial difficulties, people of below average and average intelligence did just fine when compared with the super-intelligent."

9. See endnote #3.

10. Scott I. Rick, Cynthia E. Cryder, and George Loewenstein (2008), "Fatal (Fiscal) Attraction: Spendthrifts and Tightwads in Marriage," "Tightwads and Spendthrifts," *Journal of Consumer Research*, 34 (6), 767-82; the abstract can be found at *http://ssrn. com/abstract=1339240*.

11. At the turn of the 20th century, Churchill spent 90 GB pounds per year on silk underwear. In today's 2013 US dollars, assuming 3% inflation and today's dollar to sterling conversion, that's about $2,500 per year spent on underwear. Forgive any historically inaccurate assumptions. The nub is the Old Boy spent a small fortune on his undies.

12. Robert Ferber and Lucy C. Lee (1974), "Husband-Wife Influence in Family Purchasing Behavior," *Journal of Consumer Research*, 1 (1), 43-50.

13. A painting rendered by the Boulder artist, Jane Golden, so titled: "19 & no car payments."

14. This quotation is from "Lady Windermere's Fan: A Play About a Good Woman," a four act comedy by Oscar Wilde.

15. Laura Ann McCloskey (1996), "Socioeconomic and Coercive Power within the Family;" *Gender and Society*, Vol. 10, No. 4, pp. 449-463. Men's economic vulnerability often emerges as a risk factor for domestic violence.

16. See endnote #8.

17. Robert Frank, *The High-Beta Rich: How the Manic Wealthy Will Take Us to the Next Boom, Bubble, and Bust* (New York: Random House, 2011).

18. Ron Leiber, "When Fledglings Return to the Nest," *New York Times*, July 10, 2009.

19. Brad M. Barber and Terrance Odean, "Boys Will Be Boys: Gender, Overconfidence, and Common Stock Investment;" published in the February 2001 issue of M.I.T.'s *Quarterly Journal of Economics*.

20. Marianne Bertrand, Jessica Pan, Emir Kamenica, "Gender

Identity and Relative Income within Households;" *National Bureau of Economic Research*, Working Paper #19023, Issued May 2013; *NBER* Program: *http://www.nber.org/papers/w19023*.

Wendy Wang, Kim Parker, Paul Taylor, "Breadwinner Moms;" *Pew Research Center*, published May 29, 2013; *http://www.pewsocialtrends.org/files/2013/05/Breadwinner_moms_final.pdf.*

Catherine Rampell, "U.S. Women on the Rise as Family Breadwinner," *New York Times*, published May 29, 2013; *http://www.nytimes.com/2013/05/30/business/economy/women-as-family-breadwinner-on-the-rise-study-says.html.*

21. Household Survey; *US Bureau of Labor Statistics*; Supporting narrative can be found at *http://www.nytimes.com/interactive/2013/02/08/business/Its-a-Mans-Recovery.html.*

22. *Pew Research Center*, "The Decline of Marriage and the Rise of New Families," *http://www.pewsocialtrends.org/2010/11/18/the-decline-of-marriage-and-rise-of-new-families/.*

23. This trend is evident in recent compilations of college enrollments by gender, i.e., *The Princeton Review* books on colleges. Additionally, a good article on the topic, "The Male-Female Ratio in College," by Daniel Borzelleca, February 16, 2012, can be found at *forbes.com.*

24. See endnote #22.

25. Speaking to this subject are books such as *Primal Leadership* by Daniel Goleman, Richard E. Boyatzis, and Annie McKee, and *Emotional Intelligence 2.0* by Travis Bradberry and Jean Greaves.

BIBLIOGRAPHY

Brandon, Ruth. *The Dollar Princesses: Sagas of Upward Nobility, 1870–1914.* New York: Alfred A. Knopf, 1980.

Gilbert, Martin. *Churchill: A Life.* New York: Henry Holt and Company, 1991.

Goleman, Daniel. *Emotional Intelligence.* New York: Bantam Books, 1995.

Goleman, Daniel; Boyatzis, Richard; McKee, Annie. *Primal Leadership: Learning to Lead with Emotional Intelligence.* Boston: Harvard Business School Press, 2002.

Hyde, Lewis. *The Gift: Imagination and the Erotic Life of Property.* New York: Vintage Books, a Division of Random House, 1983.

Malinowski, Bronislaw. *Argonauts of the Western Pacific.* Illinois: Waveland Press, 1984.

Manchester, William. *The Last Lion* (Volumes 1 & 2). Boston, New York, London: Little, Brown and Company, 1988.

Mauss, Marcel. *The Gift: The Form and Reason for Exchange in Archaic Societies.* New York: W. W. Norton & Company, 1990.

Soames, Mary. *Clementine Churchill: The Biography of a Marriage.* New York: Houghton Mifflin Company, Mariner Books, 2002.

Trungpa, Chögyam. *Shambhala: The Sacred Path of the Warrior.* Boston & London: Shambhala Publications, 1988.

ACKNOWLEDGEMENTS

I wish to thank my editorial team of Maria Butler and Carolyn Kanjuro. At every stage of the project they provided invaluable, keen guidance.

Gratitude of the first order goes to *the readers*, Caroline Quine and Mark Washburn. They offered persuasive critiques on the focus and flow of the essays in the manuscript.

Research studies cited in this work depended heavily on the reliable and rangy work of Lena Papadopoulos, a graduate student (at the time) in anthropology at the University of Colorado at Boulder. Her efforts and analysis are greatly appreciated.

Michael Signorella, book designer, once again rose to the challenge and displayed his left brain / right brain genius. Kudos, Michael.

Finally, there is Mr. Lewis Hyde and his oeuvre, *The Gift: Imagination and the Erotic Life of Property*. In these essays I found a framework that let me build a kindred and generative home for my own ideas. A sincere thank you to Lewis Hyde.

ABOUT THE AUTHOR

Lion Hearted Love is the second of three books on an alternative money universe—a universe that is attuned to self, psyche, spirit, and the earthy side of love and relationship … as well as money.

As for the author, he loves this money-in-relationship stuff. His work by day, as financial advisor, is quietly infused with it, and of course this collection of essays is a not-so-quiet expression of it.

At present, Mark is working on book three—a guide to how we might educate the younger generation on the subtle and practical arts of personal finance. In that vein, he also writes the blog, Enlightened Bank of Mom & Dad.

Boulder, Colorado is home for Mark and his family.

Lion Hearted Love gently lures its readers into the trenches of money-in-relationship with levity and compassion. It cuts through the illusions and limiting beliefs around finances that can destroy marriages and partnerships. I am especially grateful to Mark for acknowledging the value of the "Kitchen Sink," a metaphor representing the myriad of responsibilities required to manage a household. Wealth and abundance in relationship thrive where both partners share in the work of supporting and balancing everything!
—*Deborah Inanna Krenza, President, Gates of Inanna Ranch, Lyons, Colorado*

Mark Butler has written—simply and directly—about a topic rarely discussed: The incredibly potent part that money plays in a committed relationship. He hones in on the changing roles of each partner over the long haul, and brings a sense of sanity to how financial practicalities can be integrated. Butler helps us to return to that soft spot in our heart, again and again, as we are reminded of the love that brought us together in the first place.
—*Jonathan Barbieri, fmr. Exec. Dir., Shambhala Mountain Center*

Now here is a consummately readable book. Penned by a seasoned financial advisor, its message is delivered in the context of a provocative discourse on relationships, financial resources, and having the emotional intelligence to understand the connection between them. Mark is a delightfully thought-provoking author.
—*Robert Krenza, Founder & CEO of Black Wolf Consultants, LLC*